UPLIFT

YOUR TEAMS

LEADERSHIP LESSONS FROM LEADERSHIP SPECIALIST

ANTON GUINEA

First published by The Rural Publishing Company.

eBook: 978-0-6458801-5-1
Print: 978-0-6458801-2-0

The Rural Publishing Company
Email: hello@theruralpublishingcompany.com.au
Website: https://theruralpublishingcompany.com.au

THIS IS THE MOST IMPORTANT BOOK DEDICATION YOU WILL READ.

This is the most important book dedication you will read.

This book is dedicated to all of those leaders out there who have underperforming teams. Particularly those leaders who contact us and say that they've got a team in turmoil. Because that's a tough position to be in—the leader of a team that is still forming or storming, after years of trying to get the performing and even high-performing stages.

This book is dedicated to those leaders out there who feel like they've tried everything. They feel like there's no light at the end of the tunnel. They feel alone. They even feel anxious or depressed about the situation. Which is not a great place to be. To you, we say, stay strong; this book is designed to help you out of the current quagmire you find yourself in.

If you are one of those leaders, you'll know deep down in your heart of hearts that it's only one person on your team who's derailing the train. Who's causing the turmoil. Who's making your life hard. Two people at the very most. It's generally never more than one, but two maximum. And you can either fire them, or work with them in a way that you have haven't tried as yet. You can uplift your team, if you try hard enough. If you're committed to the uplift. And if you apply what you learn in this book.

This book is dedicated to those leaders who have high-performing teams, and want to take their teams to a point that is ever more high-performing. Go you. Great goal. Most of our work is in this space. We tend to attract leaders and teams who are skyrocketing their performance and hitting their targets. This book is for you, too!

> **I was part of a team that was in total turmoil. That was dysfunctional. I suffered through poor leadership, and I'm committed to helping the old-school leaders who are willing to learn how to uplift their teams to high performance.**

Uplifting your teams is about being willing to take a different approach. To be totally committed to better team results. To being a leader that's transformational, rather than transactional. A leader who sees humans as the solution, not the problem. A leader who wants the very best for their themselves, their team, and their organisation.

If you read the above paragraphs and are a little freaked out, don't be. You have two options: you can put this book down and never look at it again, or you can work through it, and see what happens to your team performance, and to your leadership strategy. And see what happens to your team and your team members after you apply what you've learnt.

This book is also dedicated to all of the amazing mentors, coaches and trainers, who I have learnt so much from over the years. I've invested hundreds of thousands of dollars into my professional education, not only to be the leader that my team and business needs, but so I can share what I've learnt with you—the leader who's ready to uplift their team!

Finally, this book is also dedicated to my amazing family, Mrs G (the amazing teacher), Toby (Son 1—engineer), and Zac (Son 2—future pilot) who've been on this crazy journey with me since 2004. They are my tribe, my number 1 team, and they are my motivation to be the best human and leader that I can be.

HOW TO USE THIS BOOK

This book is a playbook, not a story book.

It comprises a series of standalone ideas, elements, and tips and tricks to help you. It comes with actions to take to become a better thinker, a better leader, and a better advocate for your team's professional development. You'll also find a series of prompts and questions to encourage you to reflect honestly on your leadership skills and practices, and to think of ways to upgrade, upskill, and uplift yourself and your team.

Happy reading! You're on the way to being the best leader that YOU can be.

UPLIFT
YOUR TEAMS

WITH THE UPLIFT MODEL

This model was developed as a strategic tool for putting theory into practice to uplift your teams.

The model draws on various psychological theories relating to attitude, perception, and emotional experience in the workplace, and structures this information into a practical framework to guide leaders through the process of uplifting their teams by becoming better leaders.

It was developed over nearly 20 years of theoretical analysis combined with real-world experience, and it underpins the Guinea Group's winning formula for creating effective leaders, high-performing teams, and workplaces that are both physically and psychologically safe for workers.

Refer back to this model while reading this book. It'll help you form a concrete framework in your mind that will, over time, become a natural reference point as you grow and develop in your attitudes and behaviours, and move you closer to being the leader you want to be.

To make the most of this resource, contact us via our website at antonguinea.com.au for a self-diagnostic tool and action plan to review and improve your skills against the model.

01 UPLIFT YOUR **TEAM**
Skillset: Create a high-performing and psychologically safe team

02 FACILITATE **TEAM DISCUSSION**
Skillset: Give your team members a voice, and let them challenge you

03 ROLE MODEL **LEADERSHIP**
Skillset: Lead by example, so team members do as you say, and as you do

04 DEAL WITH **DIFFICULTIES**
Skillset: Lead your team out of turmoil and into productivity

05 DEMONSTRATE **RADICAL CANDOUR**
Skillset: Care first, and show it, before you challenge directly

CONTENTS

INTRODUCTION:
UPLIFT YOUR TEAMS

When you're uplifting your teams, you have to begin at the top of the business.

Most of our work is with the most senior leader, and their team. The leadership team. And after many years, and many clients working within senior teams, we know that there are some key things that just work when it comes to getting it right at the top of the business.

Getting it right is important at the top, because it sets the agenda for the business and everyone in it. In general terms, people are a reflection of their leaders. If you aren't sure that this is the case, and you're the GM or the CEO, try changing your languaging, and watch others change. Try being calmer in your approach, and watch what happens. It's human to mirror the behaviour of our leaders.

Hence the saying that culture is driven from the top of the business. I agree with this statement (although I think it's also changed in an upward direction, too). We work with teams that are in turmoil, and we work with teams who are high performing and want to get even better results. The same applies to both scenarios.

For senior leaders who want to uplift their team culture—and their organisational culture—here are some things to consider.

ONE PROFILE THE HECK OUT OF YOUR TEAM.

If there's one piece of advice that I'd give even the most senior of leaders, it's to start profiling your senior leaders, and don't stop. Do it regularly. I've seen senior leaders either think this isn't important, or think they're all over it already. Either way, profile and profile some more.

Use DiSC, use Resicoach, use TMS, or use whatever other profiling tool your business is comfortable with. And as part of the profiling, use your team meetings (at times) to discuss the profiles, and discuss how everyone on the team is unique. They all have their own style, and their own reasons for why they do what they do.

It's good to understand that. It's good to get into connection, and not just give direction. Take the time to understand your team and what makes them tick. Yes, they're humans, too. They're engaged to lead a department, or a unit, or a product line, but the better you know your leaders, the better they'll be able to do their jobs.

The first part of our leadership workshops is about learning (LEAD: learn, engage, articulate, demonstrate), and the learning piece is such an important element of any team. Learn about self, and learn about others.

When I say profile the heck out of it, I mean regularly. Like, bi-annually or maybe even quarterly. Profiling helps everyone on your leadership team to understand each other, and it's what makes the magic happen.

TWO WORKSHOP THE HECK OUT OF PROBLEMS.

Have idea-generation sessions. Do root-cause workshops as a team. Think critically. Challenge paradigms. Spend one hour a month working on very discrete and defined problems or decisions that only the senior leadership team can address.

And maybe even bring in some other organisational experts to work on the issues. This approach is a focused defect-elimination approach, and not only solves big problems in the business, but also brings the senior leadership team together. It creates a bond. It creates trust. If done properly, that is. With respect for each other and with the right intent.

Problem-solving workshops are not just to solve problems—they're team building workshops. They're a way for the senior leaders to connect, and to talk through things are important. The process is to schedule them, to follow up on last month's actions, and to come up with a new problem to address. Or you might address the same problem for two or three months in a row, to go deep on it.

I've seen this make a massive difference for organisations. They generate a massive return on investment, especially when driven by the most senior leader. If it's important to them, it'll be important to the leadership team.

THREE COACH THE HECK OUT OF THE SENIOR LEADERS.

Yes, as a leadership coach, I know how valuable this is for your team. The teams that I work with go from where they are to where they want to. With support. And that support might be one-on-one support for one or more of the team members, or it might be group coaching.

Our process is specifically to work with a leader, if we're doing one-on-one, and then to work with their leader. I've given up coaching leaders if their own leader is not engaged. We work with the leader, and the leader's leader. Because it works. Period.

It's nearly unreasonable not to get a leadership coach for your senior leadership team now. Businesses expect leaders to work under immense pressure. To lead large teams. To take responsibility and accountability for everything in their patch. Without anyone to support them when the times are tough, or when they need someone to reach out to.

Coaching is your security blanket. It's your drop sheet. It's your fall back position. So that not only are leaders able to learn tools and skills that they can apply during the good times, but they'll also have someone to call on during the tough times. And with coaching, some of those tough times can be avoided. Coaching is such an important element of senior leadership team success. Yes, we've gone on the journey with a heap of leadership teams, and they get huge value. And a huge return on their investment.

Learn about yourself, and others, with profiling. Take a critical thinking approach to your meetings, and workshop your team's problems on a semi-regular basis. Most importantly, get someone external to the business in your corner, someone who can support you and your team through the good times—and the tough times.

SKILL 1

UPLIFT YOUR TEAM

DYSFUNCTIONAL TEAMS SUCK. THEY REALLY DO.

I've been coaching leaders and teams now for what feels like a lifetime, and I've seen first-hand the impact that dysfunction has on team members. I've seen countless people go off on stress leave. I've seen people turn to addiction or substance abuse, and I've seen leaders that sometimes don't even know how much harm they're causing. I've even seen leaders who do.

The first time I got a call about this sort of issue, the person said something like, 'Anton, do you work with teams in turmoil?' I do now, I said. Now, many years later, my response is different. My response is simply: What's their name? Who's the person? As sure as I stand here at my stand-up desk typing, dysfunctional teams are only struggling with one person. Max two. And the leader can't work out how to lead them. Or how to lose them. Both are viable options, if the situation is bad enough. It usually isn't.

For those teams, we lean into TMS (Team Management Systems) as a profiling tool for the team, and for the team members. And we work with the leader on different strategies to engage the person. Sadly, sometimes it's the leader who's the source of the dysfunction.

The other thing we do is grab the book The Five Dysfunctions of Team by Pat Lencioni.[9] That book is an absolute winner, and we work through the five things that totally derail team performance.

Quite the negative article so far, as I reread it. Let's lighten it up a bit and get more positive. The mission is always—regardless of where a team is at—to take them to higher levels of performance.

But how do you uplift a team's performance?

ONE STEP ONE IS ALWAYS ABOUT CONNECTION.

Aiir Consulting shared some research that showed that 'Connected teams demonstrate a 21% increase in profitability over their less-connected counterparts.' This is such a simple statistic, but one that reveals so much.

But what does it mean to be connected?

> **For some, a connected team means that all team members are on the same page technologically, each taking advantage of the latest collaboration software to get work done. For others, it means a team that has deep emotional connections with each other and operates more 'like a family'. (C**redit: Jostle**)**

Both of these definitions sum up connection. It means that team members are communicating clearly, and consistently. Simple. There are strong relationships formed within the team. Team members aren't afraid to share information, they're not afraid to share bad news, and they're certainly not afraid to be vulnerable. Connected teams have high trust factor, and high morale, because with connection comes care factor.

If your team isn't performing, or can be higher performing, consider how connected they are, both online and in person.

TWO STEP TWO IS ALWAYS ABOUT TRUST.

Aiir Consulting also shared some research that showed that '45% percent of people said that a lack of trust in leadership was the biggest issue impacting their work performance'. Another simple statistic, that reveals so much.

A lack of trust also happens to be one of the five dysfunctions of a team. That's at team level. But when a team doesn't trust their leader, that can be next-level disastrous for a team and their performance. The issue with trust is that it takes a long time to gain it, and it only takes one moment to lose it.

In my experience, perhaps the saddest thing that I see is a leader throwing a team member under the bus. Or not supporting them, when it matters. And when a team member doesn't feel supported, there's only one way team's performance is heading. Sadly, it's never a one-sided situation—if you watch a team member who feels supported, they'll walk over broken glass for their leader (a bit of a blood analogy for our visual learners, sorry—just making a point). Decisions get made. Conversations get had. Communication happens, when leaders support their team members.

If your team isn't performing, or can be higher performing, consider how to increase the level of trust the team has in their leader.

THREE STEP THREE IS ABOUT PSYCHOLOGICAL SAFETY.

This is the big one.

I've written and spoken about this topic relentlessly for about three years now. This is the concept that Amy Edmondson started to make famous in 1999[5] by studying it in organisations, and Google made even more famous when they did a two-year study (Project Aristotle) that found that psychological safety was the one thing that made Google teams successful.

Yes, Google put this concept on the map. But since then, the concept has gone nuts, and there's even a guideline in Australia now that mandates how it'll be implemented in organisations. If you fail to maintain psychologically safe teams, you're now breaking the law. A big step. And a good one.

In short,

> **Psychological safety is about creating an environment where staff can speak up, share ideas, ask questions, and make mistakes without fear of humiliation or retribution. Creating this environment supports genuine participation and contribution by all staff as they feel valued and respected. (Credit: WA Gov)**

If your team isn't performing, or can be higher performing, consider how to increase the level of psychological safety in your team.

To sum it up, uplifting your team is about getting connected, getting trustworthy, and getting psychologically safe. But the work doesn't stop when you get there.

When your team is high performing, what do you do then?

THE QUANDARY OF THE HIGH-PERFORMING TEAM

The quandary for high-performing teams is: how do they get even MORE high performing? When your team is at the top of its game, how can you elevate it even further? Yes, it's a good quandary to have, but what's the solution? Glad you asked.

Luckily for our business, we've become somewhat of an expert in this area— because most of our work is with high-performing teams. I know, right? For every call we get from a team in turmoil (or a leader in turmoil), we get three calls from a high-performing team, asking for help to take them to the next level. (Which is a beautiful thing for us.)

We've often reflected, inside TGG, on why that's the case. We keep coming back to the fact that we're quite positive about life, positive about the potential of teams and their leaders, and positive in our languaging. We seem to attract more of what we put out.

The other thing we think is that it can be hard for leaders to reach out if their team is in turmoil. It's like admitting defeat. I get that, too. Just make the call—you'll be glad you did. Never be too proud or to fearful to ask for help.

But back to taking high-performing teams to the next level.

Firstly though, what makes up a high-performing team? There are a few models out there for those readers looking for the details and research behind this section. We default to the Lencioni Model (2002),[3] which includes building trust, constructive conflict, commitment, accountability, and attention to results. And yes, we could survey your team, and measure your level of achievement in each of these areas.

Let me make it simpler.

High-performing teams only do two things. They have a high level of output. This is about what they do—they get work done. And they have a high level of relationships. This is about how they do it—they get work done, while caring for each other. And while doing no harm to each other along the way.

OUTPUTS

For outputs, think measurables. Some of our clients are in the project management and construction industries, and their measurables are around safety, schedule, cost, and quality. Your outputs might be KPIs, or daily, weekly, monthly, or quarterly targets. They're the items discussed when you talk about deliverables with your team, as their leader.

RELATIONSHIPS

For relationships, think team dynamics. Think communication styles. Think empathy, and think psychological safety. Think care factor, and connection. Relationships are very intangible, and they're not as measurable as the outputs, but they have more impact on the performance of your team. How your team delivers its outputs is more important than what it delivers.

When we survey lower-performing teams, outputs are generally higher than relationships. Relationships are their area for potential improvement.

And regardless of whether the team is high- or low-performing, high outputs are not sustainable if relationships and care factor are low (you might need to reread that last sentence).

So, how do teams become even more high performing? They focus more on outputs than relationships. They're already working well together, so the question becomes 'how we can we leverage how well we work together to get more done?' A great question—as long as the team already works well together.

Because uplifting teams begins at the top of the business, what you might need to look at is increasing the bandwidth of your senior leadership team.

How To Increase Your Senior Leadership Team's Bandwidth, And Why

'Why can't we ever get anything completed?!...' a distraught senior leader asked me during a coaching session. 'As a senior leadership team, we seem to get a lot of things started, but we never seem to really see these things through to completion. It's like we hit the ground running when the starter's gun goes off, but we can't seem to finish the race. It's a never-ending cycle of incomplete action, items and projects,' the leader went on.

The leader was obviously at their wits' end, and was struggling to understand what was at play in their senior leadership team that they just couldn't create the accountability and the responsibility that's needed to complete game-changing projects.

I asked the leaders about the bandwidth of their leadership team.

That question was met with raised eyebrows, and I explained that bandwidth is just as it sounds. Bandwidth is about the breadth of skills of the team, and the senior leaders in it. Think of bandwidth like a sine wave or waveform, which has an amplitude and a frequency (and can oscillate between high or low, depending on the situation). In short, leadership bandwidth is about having broad leadership skills that are capable of dealing with a range of issues in the organisation.

The concept of leadership (even management) bandwidth is not a new one, but my personal take on bandwidth is that it's about individual bandwidth, leadership bandwidth, and organisational bandwidth.

Let me explain.

INDIVIDUAL BANDWIDTH (OF SENIOR LEADERS)

Leaders need to be flexible, and they need to adapt. The most important thing they need to adapt to is the different communication styles of the members of their teams. And if you need to understand more about this, please reach out so we can assist with DiSC profiling, to help you understand the communication preferences of your team members.

For leaders, the better they can understand communication styles, the more they can adapt to different styles.

But it's not just communication styles that they need to adapt to. Leaders need to be able to deal with internal and external stakeholders. They need to be able to talk to the cleaner with as much respect as other senior leaders.

They need to manage every conceivable emotion, and they need to do all of that with conscious control, connection, and courage.

In other words, leaders need to develop a wide bandwidth of skills to deal with various communication styles, personality styles, emotional styles, and everything in between. Leadership is a dynamic process, not a static one.

Without a wide individual bandwidth of personal interaction skills, leaders will struggle not only to connect, but to inspire others to follow through and hit their goals, objectives, and the completion of major projects.

The solution to this issue really is external leadership training and coaching, with a focus on people skills and leading under pressure.

LEADERSHIP BANDWIDTH (OF ALL LEADERS)

Leadership bandwidth (called management bandwidth by some scholars) is about the ability of the leaders in an organisation to lead their teams. That is, to do all the things that engage, energise, and enable others to aspire to greatness and to work at a high-performing level.

Leadership bandwidth starts with the senior leadership team. If they don't have the bandwidth to start, follow through, and complete projects, then things will either not get started, or not get finished. And yes, being a starter or a finisher is a personality trait.

Or the senior leaders don't provide the coaching that's needed to develop other leaders in the business to become better versions of themselves.

Or the lower-level leaders don't understand how to create a culture of completion. Of high performance. Of project delivery.

Or the lower-level leaders don't have the skill sets in their teams to deliver on the project requirements, which always require a diverse range of skills (see the next point on organisational bandwidth for more of an explanation on this point).

The solution to this issue is internal leadership training and coaching, with a focus on senior leaders supporting their leaders, and ensuring that they're developing the skills—and are given the support—to deliver on their responsibilities and accountabilities.

ORGANISATIONAL BANDWIDTH (OF ALL HUMANS IN THE BUSINESS)

Some businesses suffer with a bandwidth issue. Imagine for a moment that your project was a technology-based project, but you don't have a developer or software engineer on your team, and you don't know what to look for in a developer. Your team's chances of successfully implementing a technology project are Buckley's and none.

Or imagine that your key team members are on parental leave or long service leave for the duration of a key project. Or that the server keeps crashing when people work from home, or that the sales team has overcommitted and made promises that the operations teams cannot deliver on.

These are organisational bandwidth issues. And yes, some of these are temporary. In fact, any bandwidth issue can be viewed as temporary, if it's understood and addressed.

The solution to this issue is to put some time and effort into project planning, project resourcing, and project scheduling. Including what's realistic and what's not. And what resources are required, that aren't currently available to you and the team.

In summary, senior leaders need a wide bandwidth, due to the wide array of circumstances, situations, and humans they're required to deal with on a daily basis. Leadership bandwidth is about every leader in the business, and whether or not they're able to lead their teams to greatness. Organisational bandwidth is about the organisation's ability to deliver on major projects.

And yes, all of these helped my coaching client, though time will tell if they can get more key projects completed.

Sometimes, you might need to switch things up. Sometimes, new humans are needed to increase the bandwidth of the senior leadership team. But how do you find, and hire, the right humans?

HOW TO HIRE THE RIGHT LEADERS FOR YOUR ORGANISATION

If you want to create a nightmare in your organisation, hire the wrong leader. If you want to upset everyone, and lower morale, hire fast and fire slow. If you want to demonstrate that you're more worried about bums on seats than hiring quality leaders, hire the first applicant. Or even worse, promote someone just because they're a good technician, and not necessarily because they're a good leader.

On the other hand, if you want to hire great leaders, who care about your business, and who are aligned with your values and vision, here are my top three hiring tips.

ONE HIRE FOR VALUES.

Here's what can happen.

You're a senior leader. You hire a leader, for your leadership team. They like your organisation for a while. Then, there's a tough decision to make. Or you need them to implement a change that they don't entirely agree with. They're not happy anymore. They leave. When you ask why they left, they say very simply: 'Because my values don't align with the values of the organisation.' Ouch.

So, the challenge is, how do you prevent this process from playing out in your organisation? It's not easy, but the one thing you can do is to be very clear on values in the job interview.

In my leadership coaching sessions, I encourage senior leaders to ask applicants for their top three values, and then ask how they align with the organisational values. This will tell you if they've done that thinking around why they really want to work for you, and if they feel like you're going to be a good fit, from a values perspective. It also shows if they've done some research into your values, which is important.

LEADER ACTION

Before you ask about values, be clear on what your own values are, and what the organisational values are.

TWO HIRE FOR FIT.

The old saying is that we hire on attitude, we don't hire for skill. Yep, that used to be relevant. And it you're hiring a salesperson, or a tradesperson, or an administrator, great strategy.

But if you're hiring a senior leader, it's just not that simple. Senior leaders need to have the right attitude, and the right skills. You don't have the time or the effort to train your senior leaders to be good leaders. You'll coach them, but you just can't be running around after them, doing their job. Which will happen if you don't hire the leader that best fits into your team, or organisation, or culture.

Hire senior leaders on fit. Cultural fit. Because culture is driven from the top of the organisation, the leader that you hire will be expected to drive the culture. And you might want an inclusive culture, and engaging culture, a proactive culture, or even just a positive culture.

What's a positive work culture? Simply put, a positive work culture is one that prioritises the wellbeing of employees, offers support at all levels within the organisation, and has policies in place that encourage respect, trust, empathy, and support (Credit: Wiki).

If you get the feeling that the languaging and the behaviour of the applicant you're considering won't drive this type of culture, say to yourself: NEXT.

LEADER ACTION

Before you ask about culture (like values), be clear on what culture you're trying to drive in your business, and what you expect of your leaders in that space.

THREE USE THE COFFEE CUP TEST.

This is my favourite, and there are two stages to this one.

Firstly, be aware of how the applicant treats others, either on their way to the interview, or just as they enter the building. Ask the receptionist for feedback on how they were treated by the applicant when they arrived. If they don't treat people with respect, because that person is not seen by them as being important, that should be a red flag.

The second thing to do—this is my favourite, and I've used it on multiple occasions—is to make sure that your applicant has a coffee or a drink of water during the interview.

The kicker: watch what they do with it at the end of the interview. See if they take it back to the kitchen, or to the sink. You can tell a lot about a leader just by watching their behaviour, and it's something that most people either don't notice, or don't think is important.

LEADER ACTION

This takes no effort at all. It's about being observant. Be observant of all elements of body language, because what the leader does, the team will follow.

If you've read the first book in this series, you'll know how important it is to have a future focus in leadership, especially when you're hiring new leaders. Think about where you're taking the team and the organisation, and who'll be among the best leaders for the job.

But once you find them, how do you use them to uplift the team?

That's where systems leadership comes into play.

HOW TO USE SYSTEMS LEADERSHIP TO UPGRADE YOUR TEAM

Systems leadership was made famous by MacDonald, Burke, and Stewart,[10] in the book of the same name. That book unpacked the key elements of systems leadership and described the elements of human decision making.

Human decision making is about being charismatic, technical, and academic. Part of that decision making relates to culture and beliefs, hypotheses, and action testing.

Ultimately, it's how leaders facilitate these, and the other components of dealing with the humans in their teams (at the same time, increasing productivity and output) that's the focus of systems leadership.

As a side note, the book references the work of Elliot Jaques,[7] who authored The Requisite Organisation, which looks at layers and levels of organisations. Jaques was a psychoanalyst, who focused on organisation hierarchy and organisational structures. These are important elements of systems leadership of course, but systems leadership, to me, is more about making the job of leading a more systematised process.

And that's the reason I was compelled to write this section. Too many leaders that I speak to, and coach, struggle with time, business, and pressure. They miss the 1:1 meetings they should be attending, and they don't have the ability or the time to prioritise people. Systems leadership takes care of that. In short, it takes the people part of leadership, and turns it into a system that can be scheduled, planned, and prioritised.

So how do you do systems leadership, from the perspective of this leadership coach?

ONE   REMEMBER THAT LEADING AND MANAGING ARE BOTH IMPORTANT.

This is the key premise of systems leadership (and mind you, the topic of many blog posts and possibly books for me). For some reason, people are fascinated by the dichotomy between managing and leading—without really understanding that a great leader needs to be a great manager, and vice versa. It does frustrate me (just a little) to read post after post about leaders and managers, from people who just don't get how the two come together.

They come together in systems leadership.

In essence, people are the most important thing in a leader's life. But the challenge is that a leader's time is not their own, and they're pulled from pillar to post. They're busy humans, and they need to go to endless meetings, just to keep up with what's happening in their organisation.

So, how do they make people their priority? Simple. Diarise it. If it's important enough to attend all the other meetings in the business, it must be important enough to attend meetings with team members, right?

Here is systems leadership 101 (don't thank me now): 1) Work out what meetings (or time) you need to dedicate to your team, or your team members individually. 2) Put these in your calendar. 3) Commit to them, and never miss one or reschedule.

Voila, you've applied systems thinking to your leadership. Done. Systematise the people work that you need to do.

TWO MEASURE YOUR OUTPUTS AND RELATIONSHIPS.

Have I mentioned that we at TGG are very simple humans, and actually, we are the masters of simplification? Our business has a process for determining whether or not a team is high performing. And it's simply this.

If you look at a team, and what's required for it to simply function (not be high performing), there are two elements. Outputs: what the team does; and relationships: how the team does it.

In our experience, working with over 150 businesses over 18 years, what we know is that most teams will say that they're good at getting their outputs delivered, but they aren't great at delivering their interpersonal stuff (like connection and communication).

From a systems leadership perspective, systematise how you measure and mange this aspect of your team performance. Use KPIs to measure team performance, and use a morale meter, or similar, to systematically measure the relationships in your team.

Come up with a minimum level or performance—say, 70% for each. And then aim for 70% in each area, outputs and relationships. Create a system for understanding how your team is performing together, not just what they're achieving. Yes, a novel concept for some, but try it and watch the magic happen.

FYI, the relationship piece is way more important than the outputs piece. It's hard to have a high-performing team if they're at each other's throats constantly, regardless of whether the KPIs get hit.

THREE MAKE IT VISUAL.

How will the team know how they're progressing, from an output or a relationship perspective, if they can't see it? How will they even know what's important to you as their leader, if they can't see it?

As a leader, here's a key mantra of mine: if your team can't see it, you can't have it. Make it visual. It really is that simple.

If your team needs to guess what you're measuring, or how you're measuring it, forget it. They'll never buy into something they don't get, and they'll never care about that metric. Period.

So, how much do you make visual? Enough is the answer. Enough to ensure that key metrics, both outputs and relationships, are visible to all team members—and that it's updated regularly. Please don't put something on a wall somewhere and never go back to it. Put it up, and have stand-up meetings around it, to reinforce how important the metrics and the measures are to you, and why they should be important to your team.

Have somewhere between three and seven metrics (why this number? Because the human frontal lobes, and their working memory, and can only store three plus or minus two units of information at any one time). Three to seven is the magic number of anything. Whatever you do, make it visual. Especially when you're going through the bad weeks or months!

Systems leadership is not new. It's based on the premise that humans make decisions, and leaders facilitate those decisions. For me, this takes putting the people stuff into a system and calendar entries. Then, measure the outputs and the relationships in your team, and make the results visual.

But once you've got the system in place, how do you make it happen? And how do you make sure the right person is on the right task, at the right time?

The answer is a dirty word for some—allocation.

HOW TO DO ALLOCATION VS DELEGATION

One common senior leader challenge is doing all the work themselves and not delegating. Or even worse, micromanaging. Which is a recipe for disaster. And burnout.

But it doesn't have to be that way. When senior leaders realise that they have to be resourceful, and not the resource, their world shifts. And their leadership team, and all the teams in the business, are uplifted.

Delegation is a word that has a negative connotation for most leaders, and for their teams. It feels like they're doing something nasty to their team members. Or that it only happens when things are going badly and everyone is stressed. But it's precisely then that we need to delegate.

No one likes being delegated to. It feels abrupt, it feels aggressive, and it feels aloof. Especially when it's delivered in a delegation type of way. Which is very one-way.

Unlike task allocation, which is more of a consultative process (and a business process), that involves a discussion and agreement. It's a two-way, collaborative conversation.

Let me explain why you should allocate, not delegate.

ONE ALLOCATION IS ENGAGING.

Leaders need to assign work. They need to ask for support. They need to allocate tasks to individual team members, particularly when the pressure is on. Allocation takes time, because it's about the conversation, it's about the dialogue, and it's about the consensus.

The allocation of tasks and projects should include a conversation about why that task or project is important, what milestones need to be achieved, and when exactly those deadlines are. Your team members might even have some ideas to share about what could be modified or changed as part of the current plan. Then you get the opportunity to listen, learn, and lean into some optioneering. Engaging.

TWO ALLOCATION IS EFFECTIVE.

Allocation is most effective when delivered as part of a process. That process should outline the allocation of tasks with something like a RACI matrix (which states clearly who is responsible, accountable, consulted, and informed, about all of the activities completed by the team members). Too often, roles and responsibilities get blurred, and the term 'swim lanes' comes up (i.e., 'you need to stay in your swim lane').

Allocation is effective as a team activity, as well as a one-to-one activity. By its very nature, it spreads the work, assigns the activities, and aligns the tasks with the RACI matrix. It's effective because it creates clarity, consistency, and commitment. Team members are aware of their roles and responsibilities, and can talk to progress and project updates. Allocating activities to teams reduces ambiguity and uncertainty. It sets the team up for success, and it sets the team up for high performance.

THREE ALLOCATION IS ESSENTIAL.

With a RACI matrix in place, allocation becomes easy. If tasks need to be modified or managed in a way that's not aligned with the matrix, further task allocation is required, to walk the team through what needs to be modified and why. Having good business processes for the allocation of tasks is a key element of effective and high-performing teams. Essential.

Allocation is engaging, it's effective, and it's essential to a high-performing team and a high-performing leader. Unlike delegation, and the process of telling team members what to do, allocation is about engaging with them to help every team member know what the team is doing, and why. It might sound like splitting hairs when I unpack allocation versus delegation—but you only have to sit in a coaching session with me to see the emotional shift when we change that one word and share how it's done properly.

And it's a shift that helps the whole team, especially the C-Suite team, to be more attuned and aligned to the values and goals of the organisation.

HOW TO BE MORE ATTUNED AS A C-SUITE TEAM, AND WHY

C-Suite teams are living entities, which grow and reshape themselves over time. That growth is sometimes forced. Forced through the engagement of a new CEO, the implementation of a new change process, or the impact of a negative internal or external crisis event.

Gallup described attunement as 'the affective way a human is sensitive to the demands of a situation.' There are some subtleties in that definition. Affective means with emotional control. Sensitive means having acute awareness to the needs of others. The demands of a situation implies that your emotional state will be challenged by a range of situations (potentially major changes). These situations might be crisis events, or internal or external events, some with the potential to affect business continuity.

When these events occur, the C-Suite team need to be attuned. Having attunement therefore means to be adaptable, agile, and aware. Agility to take the organisation on a new journey, in a new direction. Adaptable to the changes that are occurring, and aware of how this might affect each team member. It means to be a team who shows up with energy, engagement, and enterprise thinking.

As a note, it would've been easy to include 'aligned' in the above paragraph. For me, alignment is a result of leadership, not a cause of it. In other words, if the attunement is in place, the alignment will take care of itself. Alignment is the by-product of attunement.

A C-Suite team that's attuned demonstrates to the organisation that all is well. That all is in control. That all is being managed in the best interests of the organisation and the best interests of the people in it.

But how do you become attuned as a C-Suite leadership team?

ONE BY STARTING WITH A GROWTH MINDSET.

Regardless of the situations you're currently facing the C-Suite senior leadership team, the biggest issues that the CEO will face are entrenched, embedded, and instilled ways of thinking and ways of leading. Aka: a low level of adaptability to anything new.

With change comes growth and with growth comes challenge. For some of the team, this growth, and the associated challenge, will be too much. It'll be too far to stretch, in terms of mindset, and in terms of the willingness to adapt to a new norm or to a new structure or strategy.

The research around having a growth mindset is over 35 years old now, and was carried out by Dr Carol Dweck to understand why some students (who were the study participants) bounced back after failure a lot quicker than others. Dweck's research[3] has since informed leader behaviours around having a fixed mindset (in short: stuck in the past), versus a growth mindset (in short: looking forward).

Leaders and teams with a growth mindset learn from their mistakes, and look to learn something from what has happened previously, to ensure that they get better results in the future. But having a growth mindset can be a real stretch for some of the C-Suite. Especially those members that are entrenched in fixed ways of thinking and behaving.

LEADER ACTION

If you want to get your C-Suite attuned and able to adapt to the situation, especially during or after a challenging period, step one is encouraging every member of the team to think forward, not backward. To think big, not small. To think growth, not status quo.

TWO BY CONTINUING WITH AN IMPLEMENTATION MINDSET.

The organisation is watching. They're waiting. And they're willing to follow. Especially if the C-Suite are ready to implement change and make the decisions necessary to be highly efficient, highly effective, and highly agile.

The entire organisation is ready for the change. They're ready to be led, and they're ready to be part of an upgraded and upskilled future state. And they generally don't want to wait. They want to get there quickly. Or, at least, they want to see steps in the right direction. They don't want to hear talk about what's going to happen. Words are cheap. They want to see action— from the top of the organisation—that demonstrates that the C-Suite is committed to organisational growth and change.

C-Suite teams that don't take action promptly following a demanding situation lose credibility, and quickly. A C-Suite team should act. Especially when the organisation knows that action is required.

The sign of progress is demonstrated by implementing changes. Not for the sake of change, and not as a knee-jerk reaction, but because it's the right thing to do given the situation. Agile decision making, and action taking, is a sign of an attuned C-Suite team. Particularly when the C-Suite are all committed to the decision, have the same languaging around it, and share the message with the business in a way that explains what's happening, why it's happening, and what the C-Suite are willing to do to make sure the change is successful.

LEADER ACTION

If you want to get your C-Suite attuned, step two is about being agile in decision making and action taking, to ensure that situations and organisational demands are addressed in a timely manner.

THREE BY FINISHING WITH AN AWARENESS MINDSET.

Let's bring that affective element into the attunement process.

In psychology, affect is a term that encompasses a broad range of feelings that people can experience. It embodies both emotions and moods.

An emotion is an intense feeling that's short term and is typically directed at a source. A mood is a state of mind that tends to be less intense than an emotion, and doesn't necessarily need a contextual stimulus. Moods last longer than emotions, from hours to days (Credit: DBT Centre).

When it comes to attunement, affect means being aware of one's emotions or moods, and ensuring that they're regulated in a way that those emotions are used for good, and not as an excuse for doing harm to humans through emotion-driven behaviour like aggression, abuse, or abruptness.

Self-awareness is the first and most important element of C-Suite attunement, as it demonstrates that all senior leaders are in control of their state. This allows them to have a level of situational awareness, and to clearly understand what the situation demands. It helps them to be aware of what the organisation is experiencing, because they're also experiencing the impact of the situation.

Leaders with high scores on the positive affect scale are perceived as being more connected and attuned not only to the situation, but also to the impact on others. With positive affect comes conscious control. With conscious control comes behavioural control. And with behavioural control comes situational control. It all starts with affect.

LEADER ACTION

If you want to get your C-Suite attuned, step three is about being in conscious control of your emotional state and the moods that you're experiencing. So you do no harm. And so that you can maintain control of yourself and the situation.

An effective and efficient C-Suite team is about attunement, adaptability, agility, and awareness. When those attributes are present, the team and the organisational alignment will increase. That alignment, the key element of highly effective SLTs, is what will uplift your team.

ACTIVITY 3.1
UPLIFT YOUR TEAM

The series of questions on the following pages will encourage you to think about what you can do to uplift your leadership team, and apply what you learnt in the last chapter to the process.

Can you think of ways to facilitate connection and trust among your team members, and with you as a leader?

Do you think you need to improve the psychological safety in your workplace? Why, or why not?

Is your team high performing? What measurable output targets (safety, schedule, cost, and quality) are you meeting or not meeting?

As a leader, are you flexible and adaptable? Why, or why not?

Do you think your leadership team shares your values, or the values of your organisation? Why, or why not?

Can you think of visual ways to help your team see how they're progressing, from an output or a relationship perspective?

Answer honestly. How well do you use allocation to share your workload with your team members?

What could you do to make your allocation more effective and engaging for your team members?

How could you improve your growth mindset? What about your implementation mindset, or awareness mindset?

SKILL II

FACILITATE DISCUSSION

IN 2004 I SHARED WITH MY AMAZING WIFE THAT I HAD QUIT MY JOB AND DECIDED TO BECOME A 'MOTIVATIONAL SPEAKER'. SHE WAS NOT OVERLY IMPRESSED.

To say the least. Especially for the first few years, when speaking work was somewhat hard to come by. Mostly because I wasn't very good at it. I hadn't really learnt how to engage an audience. Several years later (and thank you, Marc McLaren), an early mentor of mine shared that 'if you're going to get great at public speaking, the thing you need to learn is how to talk with an audience, not at an audience'. Some of the best advice I've ever received.

But what does that mean, and how does it apply to leadership?

In my humble opinion, engaging your team—really engaging them—is the key leadership skill of the future. Aka, workshop facilitation (or, in essence, good meeting management). FYI: how to masterfully facilitate a workshop or meeting is all summed up in an e-book available for download here.

Since the COVID pandemic started, we've moved online. We've moved work to home. We're still working through the great resignation. Which was quoted by several sources (MIT Sloan Management Review study, as an example) as being caused by 'Toxic Workplace Cultures'. Which is code for team members not being heard, and hence not feeling valued.

The most frequent query I get from our leadership coaching clients is why their teams have stopped making decisions, and how can I help them be decisive and act. The theory was that the 'water cooler' conversations were no longer happening, and team members no longer have anyone to bounce ideas off. Makes sense.

So how do we, as leaders, be a sounding board, or give team members the ability to share ideas and opinions in either one-on-ones or in group discussions? By facilitating great workshops and great meetings. By talking with team members, not at them. By giving team members a voice—a real voice (online or in person).

Here's how to do it.

ONE LEADERS, YOU DON'T NEED ALL THE ANSWERS. YOU NEED TO HAVE ALL THE QUESTIONS.

Leaders still tell me that they feel like they need to have all the answers.

And my first thought is, how is that humanly possible? Which I sometimes verbalise (on the rare occasions I haven't got my filter on). When leaders understand that all sources of information and knowledge are embedded in the collective experience of team members, and that it's a simple (sometimes not easy) process of asking for help, the answers will present themselves. Especially in areas like:

- Goal Setting,
- Idea Generation, and
- Problem Solving.

LEADER ACTION

Never undervalue the knowledge in your team, and how the right engagement and facilitation (workshop or meeting) will give team members the forum to share information and answer questions that you'll have as the team leader. Ask the right questions.

Back to learning how to be a better public speaker.

Great public speakers are generally great facilitators. To talk with an audience is simply to be able to 'curate the conversation.' To be able to thoughtfully choose great questions that will keep the dialogue in motion. Same with leadership. Keeping dialogue in motion is the fine art of facilitation, and the even more fine art of thinking fast and talking slow (yes, it's a learnt skill).

TWO LEADERS, THE MORE YOU LISTEN TO IDEAS, THE MORE IDEAS YOU'LL GET.

Listening to your team is key, especially when you're facilitating a workshop with a purpose. For those leaders who aren't yet adept at the fine art of facilitation, start with listening, and writing. Yes, writing. Writing things down and following up on ideas and opportunities.

You might not agree with an idea or opinion, but it gives value to your team member's input if you take the time to acknowledge them. Then you can close the loop on the idea (during the workshop or meeting), or on why the idea will or won't be implemented.

The challenge for some leaders is that they get too many ideas and opinions. I get that, too. The challenge here is to prioritise and work through what's achievable, and what's biggest bang for buck. And having the group conversational skills to articulate all of that.

LEADER ACTION

Workshop facilitation can be an exercise in creating conscious control, especially when you don't agree with ideas, or when the conversation is getting animated. Listen, listen, and listen some more to what's really being said, and listen for any underlying issues that might be showing up. You might even have to take some of that offline.

THREE LEADERS, DON'T THANK ME NOW. HERE'S THE PROCESS—AND A GREAT RESOURCE.

Part of the fine art of facilitation is following a process. The clearer the process, the better the outcome. (It's the same with most things in life, really, not just workshop facilitation.)

So here's the 5P process for facilitating great workshops:

- **Purpose**: clearly define it, and share it prior to the workshop or meeting;
- **Process**: how will the workshop be run, what resources will be used (preparation);
- **People**: who needs to be at the workshop or meeting;
- **Performance**: the fine art of facilitation, following the above steps of having great questions, curating conversation, and listening to and documenting what's said; and
- **Polish**: the close out process, to add value to the time that your team has committed to the process.

LEADER ACTION

The best leaders that I've encountered are engaging. They're conversation specialists, and they can curate a one-on-one chat with as much purpose and ease as they do in a group scenario.

I'm sharing this information because it was game changing for me when I learnt it. And just being told that facilitation matters didn't mean that I could do it well, right off the bat. It takes work, it takes practice, and like most things in life, what's worth having doesn't come easy. But as promised, you can learn more about information-driven workshops here.

If you follow the process, your team will give you answers, and they'll give you ideas. But that depends on an important thing: are you willing to let them contribute? Or are you going to keep micromanaging?

'IF YOU WANT SOMETHING DONE, YOU HAVE TO DO IT YOURSELF' IS SO 1900s

I went from being a stressed leader to a calm leader by working out that I couldn't do everything myself. And that I didn't have to.

My team is capable, and courageous. They can do things that I can't and shouldn't be doing. And they do them well.

Let me share with you how I learnt to trust my team—so you don't have to keep stressing out about your workload.

ONE SHORT-TERM TIME FOR LONG-TERM DIME.

Most leaders would be ready for me to write 'short-term pain, long-term gain.' But I just don't think that putting time into your team and coaching them is pain. It might be inconvenient for you at the time, but it's certainly not pain. And the dime bit refers to the return on investment that you get for the investment of your time into your team's skill set.

Take a coaching approach to your team's work. Most leaders will tell me they're time poor—and then they take on more work, instead of delegating.

LEADER ACTION

Understand that coaching your team to be able to do a task every time from now on is an investment, and one that will get you a great return. It WILL reduce the pressure on you, and on them.

TWO YOU'LL BUILD YOUR CREDIBILITY, AND TRUST IN YOU.

Trust is a beautiful thing. It's a self-fulfilling prophecy: the more trust you give, the more you get. Being trustful is good for your credibility, as your team sees you having faith in their skills and abilities. And it's an integrity thing. When you say you'll trust your team, and then follow through on that, you're winning.

Say it, then do it. Integrity and credibility are two halves of the same apple. And trust is the core that holds them together, and the core that holds your team together. Two-way trust.

LEADER ACTION

Step into being a trusting and trusted leader. Make the call to allow your team to shine or learn. Be of high integrity, and in doing so you'll reduce the pressure on you, and on them.

THREE IT ANNOYS YOUR TEAM WHEN YOU DO THEIR WORK FOR THEM.

Seriously! We can tend to think as leaders that we're helping (or at least, that's how some leaders justify dealing with stress and pressure). 'I'll help' is like having your two-year-old 'helping' you take the rubbish out. It feels good in the moment, but doesn't really add much value. In fact, it does more harm than good. And sure, you might be quicker, or better, at that task, but think about your team members for a moment. What does your behaviour say to them? I'd spell it out, but I think it might be self-explanatory.

LEADER ACTION

Understand that doing your team's work is not cool, or quicker. It's disheartening for them. Support your team if they need it. Reduce the pressure on you, and on them.

And yes, it does take conscious control to delegate tasks in the right places, and to move past the old thinking of doing it yourself. There are so many better ways to lead in this day and age, that will uplift instead of hinder your team. And your team members want to contribute—that's their greatest need on planet earth!

But what happens when you give them the space they need, and something goes BOOM? And how do you deal with team members who go BOOM when something goes BOOM?

DEALING WITH A TEAM MEMBER WHO GOES BOOM WHEN THINGS GO BOOM

Is there anything more challenging for a leader than a team member who's explosive, and who goes BOOM when the pressure comes on? This is a situation covered a lot in coaching conversations, because it's real, it happens, and it needs to be managed. With control, of course. And care factor. And courage.

One of our coaching clients (R) recently encountered this situation, and at the end of this section, I'll let you know exactly what changed his life, and why. But he had to go on a little journey to get there.

Let's unpack the process using a real-life example.

ONE DON'T IGNORE IT.

The important thing to do is to be upfront about the situation. When a team member goes BOOM, leaders need to address it straight away. If it happens in a team situation, you can address it in that forum if you're comfortable to do that. Otherwise, take it offline, and have a one-on-one conversation.

That conversation should be about unpacking what's going on for the team member, and what was driving the behaviour (care factor first). If there are other issues at play, offer support. If it's a lack of control, and going BOOM is the team member's M.O. (which it was in R's case), read on.

TWO DON'T PRESUME THEY KNOW.

Don't presume that the team member knows what they look or sound like (which is generally very ordinary). If they don't know how they're being perceived, share it with them. Share what it looks and feels like to you as their leader, and to their team (this was the case with R). Be honest with them. Be courageous enough to lay it out.

If they know, but don't care, that'll require a whole other conversation. One that's about expectations, and commitments around behaviour change.

THREE DON'T GO BOOM.

The human species has mirroring neurons, and these neurons mean we mirror the emotional state of other humans. Someone goes BOOM, we go BOOM. But that can't happen if you want to model the right behaviour and diffuse a BOOM situation.

I promised to share the secret sauce that R worked out was the big ticket item, and the one thing that changed R's life and the behaviour of that one team member.

R learnt to breathe, and to stay in control. R created conscious control. R controlled his emotions. Which meant he was in control of the situation. It was a top-shelf outcome. And if you ask R now, he'll say it's about breathing. Breathe and respond. Don't react.

In short, R is a perfect example of how to demonstrate control, care factor, and courage. And it resulted in a successful outcome for R and his team, and you can uplift yours in the same way—with conscious control.

And positive communication. Now's the time to ask yourself: are you uplifting your team by facilitating positive discussion, or are you hindering them by being part of the 'deficit dialogue dilemma'?

ARE YOU PART OF THE 'DEFICIT DIALOGUE DILEMMA'?

Maybe there are times when all you can think about is the things you don't have. The deficits. Just ask Aussies about their life, and they're always 'not bad' or 'not great'. They have no time, or not enough minutes. They're doing not much or not a lot. Which is not great as a conversation starter, and even worse as a leader, when we've got no wins, no runs on the board, no clients, or no success to celebrate.

And yes, there are leaders who are in deficit mode. Deficit dialogue is a thing. Now that you know about it, you'll start to notice it, and I'm going to note that I'm noticing it more in recent times, than in the past...pandemic maybe? Or leaders are just not choosing their language well?

So, what's the opposite of deficit? Surplus, maybe? Or abundant, or adequate, or plentiful (none of them rhyme with dialogue, though). Let's use the word 'positive'. And no, this is not just a positive thinking section, it's a positive dialogue section. It's about using language—leader language, more specifically. Which is important, because it sets the mood, and it sets the culture for your team.

The more that speak is deficit, the more that deficit shows up. And the more that deficit shows up, the more your team will focus on deficit. Or what they don't have or haven't achieved. Instead of what they do have or have achieved. It's a self-fulfilling prophecy.

Deficit dialogue can show up in one-on-ones; it can show up in team meetings; it can even show up in written communication. It's a big deal, because it instantly changes the mood or the tone of the conversation, and even of the culture of the team or organisation.

And it can become habitual. Then, one day, you'll ask yourself (or your coach, when you're sitting with me) why everyone is so negative all the time.

Here are some strategies that you can try if you're caught in the deficit dialogue dilemma. Sadly, none of them are new or groundbreaking— but they remain current, and useful, for changing the mood of your conversations, or your team.

ONE START WITH CELEBRATING SUCCESS.

This is an easy one. And in any good meeting, it's the first agenda item (or it should be). Start with a positive, and some recognition of personal or team achievement. Too fluffy for some leaders, but essential for all teams and team members (high performing ones, at least). This is also the first thing to get dropped from the agenda, when we have 'bigger fish to fry.'

TWO CONTINUE WITH SOME SOLUTIONS.

Lots of people, leaders included, have got lots of problems for every solution and not a lot of solutions for problems. As a leader, be firm on your commitment to talk in solutions and steer the conversation around to what you have to do to move forward, instead of looking back. This is a skill set.

THREE FINISH WITH SYMBOLS.

Remember that everything you say, and do, makes a statement. Know what your body language is doing and ensure that it lines up with your words. This is called being congruent. Incongruence is saying one thing, and either meaning another, or worse—doing another thing. Your team will see right through you. And no, you can't hide what you're thinking. Too many people think they can, and they end up sending the wrong message.

Other symbols include making a commitment to avoid deficit dialogue. Or rewarding positive results in general. Yes, there are times when we need to address a deficit. I get that. It's not every conversation, though. Make a commitment to surplus speaking, and see how it uplifts your team.

Then it's time to move on to another way of facilitating discussion. One that's so uplifting, it's worth more than gold.

HOW TO APPLY THE PLATINUM RULE OF COMMUNICATION

Most people have heard of the Golden Rule. Which is the principle of 'treating others as we would like to be treated.' This is a simple premise that was first noted in the big book that was penned several thousand years ago, and which contained a range if parables and testaments that were designed to help us live a more compassion-filled life.

And the Golden Rule is as current now as it was when it was first written. Imagine if everyone on the planet really bought into the Golden Rule and applied it in their own lives, and treated everyone how they would like to be treated. Yes, that's drawing a long bow, but it's a nice thought, right?

Here's another thought—when it comes to leadership, and leading under pressure, your team members don't actually want to be treated how you want to be treated. I know...breathe...

They want to be treated how they want to be treated. Yes, every team member has different requirements and a different communication style— and they'd prefer that you communicated with them in their style (not yours). This is called the Platinum Rule.

The Platinum Rule is about personal connection and productive relationships. It's about communicating in a way that's meaningful to the other person, and it's about understanding their style so that you can adapt yours. And although you change your style, you don't have to change your personality. You don't have to roll over and submit to others. You simply have to understand why people communicate how they do and understand your options for increasing the effectiveness of your communication with them, so that you can better connect. After all, communication should be for connection, not just direction.

But how do you know what someone else's communication style is? Great question, and glad you asked.

We use a personality profiling tool call DiSC, which some of my readers will be familiar with. DiSC stands for Dominant, Influential, Steady or Conscientious. From the DiSC Profile site, here are what the four personality and communication styles refer to:

- **Dominant**: A person primarily in this DiSC quadrant places emphasis on accomplishing results and 'seeing the big picture.' They're confident, and sometimes blunt, outspoken, and demanding;

- **Influence**: A person in this DiSC quadrant places emphasis on influencing or persuading others. They tend to be enthusiastic, optimistic, open, trusting, and energetic;

- **Steadiness**: A person in this quadrant places emphasis on cooperation, sincerity, loyalty, and dependability. They tend to have calm, deliberate dispositions, and don't like to be rushed; and

- **Conscientiousness**: A person in this DiSC quadrant places emphasis on quality and accuracy, expertise, and competency. They enjoy their independence, demand the details, and often fear being wrong.

Part of doing your DiSC profile is understanding how to communicate with each of the different styles. There's a great page in the profile booklet that unpacks the dos and the don'ts of each style, and how to better connect with them. How to apply The Platinum Rule, essentially.

For a leader, this information really is priceless. It cannot be overestimated how valuable it is for a leader to really understand how their team members want to be communicated with. This is especially true for new team members, who we don't know yet. Or that one team member that we haven't quite connected with.

Our leadership workshops include DISC profiling and helping leaders and team members to firstly understand their own style, and then understanding others' styles, so they can be more effective in their interactions.

The aha! moments that leaders and teams experience when they start to understand themselves and others at a different level is amazing to watch. That's when we get to see how The Platinum Rule helps to facilitate discussion, and how uplifting it is to the team.

Once you've learned the tools of facilitating discussion, you can use them right to the end of your entire leadership journey—including when it's the end of a team member's employment.

HOW TO SEND TEAM MEMBERS OFF THE RIGHT WAY

I didn't have many jobs before I quit work to start my own business. When I think back on the roles I did have, the two periods that I remember most are the engagement period and the exit period. Basically, when I started, and when I finished. And more importantly, how I started, and how I finished.

To me, these are the two most important periods of the employment tenure. And yes, there are many positive and negative times that you remember about your experiences in organisations, but how you come in and go out of an organisation is important. And the experience is driven by your leader.

Spare a thought for the Twitter staff who are or have been 'freed up for industry' by Elon Musk. Think about the excitement that they would have felt starting their employment journey with a global organisation. Then, think about what they would have experienced as they were fired by email, or by Twitter post. Imagine how those employees would feel about their experience of being let go.

I once had a manager who said that it's just as important to send team members off the right way, as it is to bring them into the organisation the right way. And I agree with that. But I understand that it's a challenge. I get that team members are usually leaving leaders, not businesses, so when team members do leave, it can hard for the leader to stay positive, and focus on providing a good leaving experience. Especially if the employment has been ended prematurely, by termination.

Here are some tips to facilitate discussion to send team members off in a professional and caring way.

ONE MAINTAIN THE RELATIONSHIP UNTIL THE END.

If the relationship is still intact when the decision is made (by you or the by the team member) to end the employment tenure, do what it takes to maintain it until the very end. Be personable, be professional, and be approachable. No matter what.

Find a way to practice what Deepak Chopra[i] calls Emotional Freedom. Which means to be emotionally free. Which is about being free of guilt, resentment, grievances, anger, and aggression. Emotional freedom is accepting the situation, whatever may have led up to it, and moving forward. Reframe the situation, find the positive, and carry on regardless.

Most team members need to provide between two and four weeks of notice and work this period after they've submitted their resignation. As a team member, that period is painful, and in my experience, most team members mentally check out. For the leader, not only do you need to be scrambling to replace the position, but you also need to be dealing with a team member who hasn't only formally resigned, but has mentally resigned too. Be patient, be accommodating, and be ready to support the departing team member, as well as your other team members during the notice period.

TWO DO AN EXIT INTERVIEW.

This is such a key step in the process of ending an employment agreement with someone, but it needs to be done properly.

It needs to be done by another person in the business, probably HR (if they've been adequately trained in doing exit interviews, because like everything, it's a skill set). The skill is related to creating a safe space for the team member to say what they really think. To give us all the good. And to give us all the bad. So you can work on improving the organisation for the next time you're ready to hire someone.

As a leader, have the courage to ask the person doing the exit interview to focus on the LMX (leader team member exchange). Ask the interviewer to focus on the relationship that the team member had with their leader. And what their experience of being led by you was like. This is crucial information, as it can determine what you could and should be doing differently as the team leader.

If this section scares you, revert to point one, and detach emotionally. Regardless of whether the team member was in your in-group or out-group, you need to hear what their experience was. You might not think that you do, but if you're open minded, and the interview is open and honest, you'll get some tips to work on as a leader. And who doesn't want that?

The message is to get the exit interview done properly, to have it focused on your leadership, and to be willing to get the feedback from that interview and integrate it into your leadership style.

THREE MAKE IT AN EVENT.

Bring in a cake. Buy muffins. Bang out some donuts. Do a morning tea. Do something special. Make it an event for the team member, so that they get the chance to celebrate the moment. Which most people want to do, regardless of the reason for their departure.

It's so uncool when leaders just let people leave without an event of some sort. Or a speech or a few kind words. Because it's not about you as the leader, it's about the team member. They want to say goodbye to their team members, they want to know that they were valued, and they might even want to have the opportunity to say thank you for the experience of working with you and the team. Never deprive a team member of the chance to say goodbye and to be farewelled in the right way.

The message is that a small event on the team member's last day will send them off the right way. They'll get the chance to end on a positive and with their head held high. They'll maintain their dignity and their self-esteem.

Put as much time and effort into helping someone leave as you do helping them join the business. How handle the exit process will say more about you as a leader than it'll say about them as a team member.

Facilitating discussion around leaving is important—even when it's only for the business's holiday break.

HOW TO CLOSE THE YEAR OUT AS A SENIOR LEADER

I've tried everything as a business owner at year's end. We've closed early, we've worked right up to Christmas Eve, we've done something in between. All the while with a focus on our team, and our clients. Our clients are generally flexible, so it's easy enough to make timing work with them.

Our staff are flexible, too. Everyone is keen to break, while at the same time knowing that we can still hustle for a few more days. Because I never really stop hustling. And I'm more in the Gary Vee School, where no one loves your business as much as you do. I get Elon's strategy of sacking people that aren't working twenty-four hours straight, but that doesn't seem right. Just because the owner wants to hustle, doesn't mean everyone has to.

In saying that, the leader needs to finish the year off well. And properly. Yes, we only have a small team that's been up and down over the years.

But here's what I've learnt over time about facilitating communication during the year-end process, and what leaders should keep in mind.

ONE DON'T OVERDO THE PARTY.

Regardless of the size of your team, the Christmas party (or end of year party—whatever your terminology is) can get out of hand.

Remembering that the Christmas party is a work function, the things that happen at the party are actually happening at work. Add alcohol, which increases the risk factor, and watch things go horribly wrong. You might get lucky, and nothing bad happens. But if it does, what's talked about at that party could be talked about in the office for the next few years, and there are just some things co-workers don't need to know about each other.

As a leader, by all means, celebrate the year and the wins with a party—just do it at lunch time, or in a more controlled way. Set some ground rules, finish the party at a reasonable hour, and never ever let anyone drive home. A wild party isn't worth the risk. You won't forgive yourself if something happens.

TWO CELEBRATE THE BUSINESS SUCCESSES.

Over the course of a year, there will be massive wins to celebrate, so celebrate strong. Thank everyone for their efforts and contributions. Congratulate them for their successes. Share the excitement of another successful year with your staff.

Review the goals that you set for your business or your team, and talk about what worked and went well, what didn't, and what you'll change into the new year. And include the team in your review. After all, they were the ones responsible for the team's success.

As a leader, remember to thank your clients. Send Christmas cards, send personal notes, send Dan Murphy's vouchers (not to government-owned corporations—be aware) and be generous. Remember that you don't have a business without clients, or a team without team members.

THREE PLAN YOUR HOLIDAY OR DOWNTIME.

This is the big one. Plan your Christmas holiday. Travel, read, take downtime. Go to the beach, unwind, and let your hair down (if you still have some).

This is a big deal for me. My wife and I try to get away every January and take at least one or two weeks where we go overseas and go touring. Recently, we visited orangutans in Borneo. We went to Borneo for two weeks to see some of the wild animals in that country with the goal of unwinding, unworrying, and unburdening.

Fun fact: Researchers have discovered that humans and orangutans share approximately 97% of their DNA. This compares to about 99% sequence similarity between humans and chimps. The orangutan is the third non-human primate to have its genome sequenced, after the chimp and rhesus macaque (Credit: National Institute of Health).

However you do it, enjoy your end of year!

ACTIVITY 3.2
FACILITATE DISCUSSION

Take some time now to think about what you've learnt in the last chapter.

The series of questions on the following pages will encourage you to assess how effective you are in facilitating discussion with your team members, and in helping them find ways to contribute positively to the team and the organisation. It can also help you to generate ideas about how you can better facilitate discussion in the process of uplifting your team.

Alternatively, spend some time thinking about how you can better create a work environment conducive to cooperation. Thinking about how you can better assist your team members to communicate and participate in the workplace will go a long way to strengthening you as an inspiring and supportive leader for your team.

Answer honestly. Do you listen to the ideas of your team members? Why, or why not?

When facilitating workshops, how well do you adhere to the 5 Ps (Purpose, Process, People, Performance, Polish)?

Answer honestly. Do you still believe that if you want something done right, you have to do it yourself?

Do you have a team member who goes BOOM when things go BOOM? How do you address it, and how can you do this better?

What practical ways can you help to overcome the deficit dialogue dilemma?

Do you understand the different needs and communication styles of your team members? How can you better address or employ them?

How do you think DiSC profiling could benefit your team and your organisation?

How do you send your team members off? Do you maintain a relationship to the end, or simply close the door?

In what ways can you better conduct exit interviews? Are there any important elements missing from this process?

What business successes can you plan to celebrate when closing out this year of work?

SKILL III
ROLE MODEL LEADERSHIP

YOUR TEAM MEMBERS ARE ALWAYS WATCHING AND LISTENING TO YOU.

What you do matters to them, and it affects how they perform in the workplace. Every one of your actions has the potential to help, harm, hear, or hurt your team members.

They're looking to you for guidance in the quiet times, during crisis events in their private lives, and even during crisis events in your life. They're looking for predictability—even when you're under the pump.

So how to you guide your team in times when your leadership matters the most? And what leadership skills do you need to uplift your team, and turn them into a high-performing people machine even during BOOM events?

WHEN LEADERSHIP MATTERS THE MOST

On August 5, 2010, a mine cave in trapped 33 miners 700 metres underground. It would take 17 days for rescuers to establish communications with the trapped workers (with a note taped to a drill bit). That note said 'We are well in the shelter, the 33 of us.' It would take 70 days for the miners to be rescued.

Luis Urzúa (54) was the shift foreman at the time of the mine cave in. Immediately following the incident, Urzúa took control. He got his team to a safe location, he managed the few resources that the team had, and he worked closely with the rescuers to evacuate the 33 miners.

But what did Urzúa do, specifically, to lead that team through such a dire situation right to the end?

'It's been a bit of a long shift,' foreman Urzúa joked. A man whose levelheadedness and gentle humour is credited with helping keep the miners under his charge focused on survival during their 70-day underground ordeal, Urzúa kept his cool in his first audio contact with officials on the surface. He glossed over the hunger and despair he and his men felt, saying, 'We're fine, waiting for you to rescue us.' (Credit: Wiki)

A mine cave in is a situation when strong leadership is required. It's an example of when leadership matters most.

ONE · LEADERSHIP MATTERS MOST DURING MAJOR CRISIS EVENTS.

Crisis events mean different things to different leaders. My definition is 'an event (or series or events) that results in a risk manifested, that causes or has the potential to cause the loss of psychological or physical safety in an organisation, or the loss of business continuity for the organisation.' I know, way too technical, but it summarises the concept.

It's during these events that our teams need strong leadership. Think Dreamworld (2016), COVID-19 (2020), and CS Energy (2021) as examples. Imagine for a moment being at Dreamworld on the day of that tragedy.

In your team or your business, a crisis event could be the economy tanking, your business struggling, or an injury or fatality on your site.

During crisis events, emotions are high, and our teams are in a state of panic. As leaders, we need to remain in conscious control, and we need to take a leaf out of Urzúa's playbook and remain calm and in control. The simple strategies that you can use to stay in control include breathing, counting to ten, and reframing the situation. Yes, they sound simple, but they work a treat—don't discount them until you've tried them!

LEADER ACTION

Because crisis events are risks manifested, you can do some preparation work to help you and your team be ready for such eventualities. Regardless, no matter how much prep work you do, as a leader you'll still need to stand up during times of crisis. Your team needs you to.

TWO · LEADERSHIP MATTERS MOST DURING TEAM MEMBER CRISIS EVENTS.

Your team members have all got personal lives. They're having experiences on a daily basis that challenge their ability to cope and to function. These situations can be overlooked by leaders in relation to their importance, but have no doubt that it's how leaders support their teams during their personal crises that demonstrates the character and values of the leader.

The very best leaders understand that if their team members are struggling, it's time for the leader to step up. And step into empathy and care factor. To understand what the team member is experiencing, and be willing to support them through it.

Whether it's the death of a loved one, the death of a pet, a cancer diagnosis, or some other personal crisis event, team members will have times when they just can't be at their best. And that's part of leading a team.

Empathy is the most important tool in the leader's toolkit during these times. Empathy requires the leader to think about what it would be like to be going through the same thing. Empathy requires an emotional connection with the team member, and it takes compassion. Compassion is about taking action to support someone. That might include reducing someone's responsibilities for a period, providing time off, or reducing their hours. I'll give you a little tip here: the leadership that you display during these times for your team members will never be forgotten (the leadership response will be internalised by your team members, because they're going through such an emotional time).

LEADER ACTION

Make sure that your team members remember how much you supported them, not how much you neglected them, during their personal crisis events. Spend a moment or two, now, reflecting on how you could demonstrate empathy, the next time you need to.

THREE LEADERSHIP MATTERS MOST DURING LEADERS' CRISIS EVENTS.

This point is one that can be quickly and quietly overlooked. Leaders are just expected to get up, dress up, and show up, regardless of what's happening in their own lives. The old rule is that leaders can't show any emotion; they need to 'take a teaspoon of cement' and get on with it, because they have work to do and a team to lead.

This is an interesting approach, and one that's partially true, but it forgets that leaders are human, too. The reason that these are the most important times for leaders to be in control is because when leaders aren't thinking clearly, they don't make great decisions. They make mistakes. I've seen leaders having to step out of their role (for a period, or forever) during these times. And that can be the right thing to do—for the leader and for the team. Making a bad decision during a tough personal time is not an excuse.

If you're a leader, and you're struggling personally, reach out for help. Let your team know what's happening for you (if you can share it) and get into coping mode. Coping mode requires you to take a problem-focused approach to your crisis (getting into action, and getting it sorted out as best you can outside of work). Take an emotion-focused approach (where you reduce the negative emotions you're experiencing, by reframing the situation) or taking an avoidant approach (not a great approach, but it might work for some crises).

Some leaders need to lean into some personal development during these times. That helps the leader to process what's happening for them, and it helps them to refine their coping skills.

LEADER ACTION

The next time things go BOOM for you, remember Luis Urzúa. And remember how he was able to remain calm, to keep 33 others calm, and how he followed his team out of a collapsed min3 after seventy days of coping with a major crisis event.

Your team members are looking to you for guidance. Unfortunately, they're sometimes also looking to you to see what they can get away with. That's when it's critical do say, and do, what you expect them to.

DO AS I SAY, AND DO AS I DO

Why do some leaders still not understand that team members don't listen as much as they watch? Why don't leaders realise that they're always on show? They're being analysed for how to behave, and their example is the most important thing that they have to influence others.

We had a client that was big on 'do as I say, not as I do.' Seriously. Their belief was that it was OK to say one thing and do another. Which is OK, if you want your team to be totally confused about the standards you're trying to maintain.

We've used this story as a case study in the past, as this leader went from being incongruent (saying one thing and doing another) to really understanding what it takes to lead by example.

Here's what she learnt.

ONE TEAM MEMBERS ARE WATCHING YOU ALL THE TIME.

This leader didn't get the importance of the behaviour that she was exhibiting. There was a lack of understanding that team members directly reflect the example of their leader. It wasn't until we were unpacking specific examples of team behaviours that it became clear just how much impact her example was having on the team—a massive learning.

When leaders get this message (emotionally, I mean; like, 'feel' it), they can be clear on the standards that they're setting. Which might be lower than they're trying to set. There's nothing like a deep understanding of 'behavioural impact' to help you out of incongruency.

TWO WHAT YOU WALK PAST, YOU CONDONE.

This was another area we worked on. Being willing to clearly set an expectation and stick to it—and hold others accountable. It's difficult to turn the incongruency ship around, but not impossible. It takes effort, and it takes honesty. And it takes being willing to call out behaviour that's not aligned with the right values or standards.

The challenge is that team standards drop to the lowest level demonstrated by one team member. And it's about having caring conversations (not robust conversations) that unpack why a certain type of behaviour is inappropriate—especially when it comes to attaining and maintaining psychological safety.

THREE DON'T DO SOMETHING THAT YOU DON'T WANT YOUR TEAM TO DO.

It's actually pretty simple.

At the end of the day, it's about integrity. The opposite of incongruence. When you say you're going to do something...do it. Follow through. That's integrity. (Aka: the most important leadership character trait, according to most team members.)

And when you've got integrity, you can role model leadership in one of the most important ways: leading to help and hear, not harm and hurt.

HELP NOT HARM, HEAR NOT HURT

I was recently in Perth speaking at the *AusIMM International Mining Conference*. Being back in WA gave me an opportunity to reflect on my time in mining there, and what I learnt from those experiences. And the thing that keeps coming up for me is that in the teams I worked in, we wanted to be heard by our leaders.

My mining career started at the ripe young age of 21. I was a young tradie who had just been released from a burns unit after more than a month of healing from a BOOM event. In the burns unit, I remember making the decision that I wouldn't be working as an electrician for any longer than I absolutely had to. That meant I needed to find something else to do with my career, and find it fast.

So, when the 'Employee Representative Role' came up, to represent the workforce in the workplace agreement negotiations, I jumped at it. A side note: this section will trigger some people in the mining industry, because it's about workplace agreements, and not unions.

For whatever reason, I've never been part of a union. Not because I didn't want to, just because I've always ended up on sites that weren't unionised, and that were termed something like 'WPAs' (aka: workplace agreements). Robe River was one of those sites.

Back to the story. My role in the process was to meet with the trades teams and get their feedback on what they were prepared to negotiate on, and what they weren't. What conditions they were chasing, and what wasn't important to them. Then, to communicate that to the management team.

And because I've never been part of a union agreement negotiation, I can't speak from that experience. I can only speak from the experience that I had, which was really very positive. It was a cool role to be put in at such a young age, and I loved every minute of it. It was my first taste of what it's like dealing with senior leaders in mining. Yes, they were tough, but they listened, were open to ideas and open to negotiation (within reason).

It was a lifetime ago, but I still have such positive memories of sitting in the equivalent of the boardroom on that mine site talking with senior leaders about the conditions for all the trades teams. And I remember constructive conversation. Not arguing or shouting. It was a calm process that required giving a bit and getting a bit.

There were other representatives, from other sections of the mine, like operations, and technical. Overall, it was a predominantly positive experience (some of the tradies gave me a hard time about not getting us enough money—to be expected), but the leaders were great to deal with. We always felt heard. We were left feeling that the WPA was helping us, not hindering us (and I must say that I could never understand how people could whinge about working in mining, when our conditions and pay were so good—even back then).

Looking back on that particular experience, it's left a lasting impact on how I approach some of the coaching sessions that I do now with leaders. Regardless of the situation, team members just want to be heard. They want to be helped. It's not just about productivity or getting the job done, it's about psychological safety. Team members that are not heard are hurt.

Leaders, always remember to help, not harm. Hear, not hurt. Yes, that's not always possible; but let it be your default position. Be consistent enough in it that you're predictable—and just a little boring.

HOW TO BE OK WITH BORING

I couldn't work out how one of my clients just kept their stuff together. Always. Never lost it. Ever. So cool, calm, and collected. Unlike me (at times). My emotions seem to fluctuate wildly, and I feel like I get the full human experience, going through all the emotional states.

So, I asked my client what was going on for them. Even when things were going south. When things weren't right. When things weren't ideal.

After some considered reflection, my client said that in their mind it was as simple as 'being OK with boring.'

Quite the insightful response. Quite the measured response. Quite the unexpected response.

I asked him to clarify it for me. He said, as a leader, you don't need to be all over the place. You don't need to be inconsistent, and you don't need to be unpredictable. You just need to be boring (not as a human), but as a leader.

Here's what else we discussed.

ONE LEARN TO BE PREDICTABLE IN YOUR EMOTIONS.

In short, don't be the leader whose team have to wait until you're in the right mood to approach.

Don't be the leader whose team have to worry about your emotions being out of control when they deliver bad news.

Don't be the leader who's unstable, unpredictable, or unreliable emotionally.

Be boring. Get in control of your emotions so that regardless of the situation, you're able to 'take it in your stride.' You're able to engage your frontal lobes and talk yourself down before responding. You're able to name your emotional state, which is the first step in the emotional intelligence process (Credit: Daniel Goleman[6]).

TWO LEARN TO BE PREDICTABLE IN YOUR BEHAVIOUR.

When we survey team members (or leaders) and we ask them what's the most important character trait that they'd like to see in their leaders, there are several commonly used words (like charisma, care factor, consistency, commitment, or communication).

What would you answer to the question of what's the most important leadership character trait? The most common response we hear is consistency. Consistency of response. Consistency of mood, and consistency of behaviour.

Team members need leaders to behave consistently. Why? Because leadership behaviour is reflected by team members. Leadership behaviour becomes the example to follow. Leadership behaviour has an impact on others. Leaders need to have the courageous conversations at times. And they need to have those in a way that's not aggressive, abusive, or abrupt. If they're any of these things, the conversation is not courageous, it's counterproductive.

Be boring. Be the leader who is so consistent that your team knows what your decisions will be before they ask you. Be the leader who has words or phrases that you use consistently. Be the leader that's in control of their behavioural patterns.

THREE LEARN TO BE PREDICTABLE IN YOUR FOCUS.

Too many leaders have too many priorities. Too many leaders are chasing their tails. Too many leaders have a daily focus instead of a monthly, quarterly, or annual focus.

One of our favourite clients picks a focus for every year. This year it was simply 'happiness'. Be happy at work. Be happy at home. Be happy at life (as much as you can—not always achievable, but a great goal). Every month, my sessions with that team are focused on content that supports the mission critical focus of happiness.

When working with that team, it's pretty simple. Is what we're doing making us happy? Is what we're doing making our team happy? Is what we're doing making our clients happy? If not, it's time to change something.

Be boring. Have a consistent focus. Have a consistent priority list. Have a consistent approach to delivering your priorities. Have punctuality (watch how much your credibility increases, just with that small change).

In summary, be boring (if I haven't mentioned that already). Yes, leadership is about firefighting. And most leaders get some excitement from reacting, rather than responding. But the more boring and consistent you can be, the better your team will respond.

Being predictable is a good thing. It means you've got the conscious control to ensure your actions are serving and positively influencing others, rather than hurting them—just like in the story of the Old Man and his Grandson.

THE OLD MAN AND HIS GRANDSON IS A LEADERSHIP STORY

Have you heard of Cinderella? Have you heard of Rapunzel? Have you heard of Snow White? Me too. But have you head of The Brothers Grimm?

Jacob and Wilhelm Grimm were two brothers that wrote the fairy tales (in the early 1800s) that we still get enjoyment from today. Their original works were quite dark, even violent, and some of those stories have been rewritten to soften them up a little. But every one of their fairy tales has a great message, and messages that are relatable and relevant to us all...in a fairy tale kind of way.

Just like the tale of *The Old Man and His Grandson*. As you read this tale, think about who you are in the story—and more specifically, how important your behaviour is and what it's saying about you.

> There was once a very old man, whose eyes had become dim, his ears dull of hearing, his knees trembled, and when he sat at the table, he could hardly hold the spoon, and spilt the broth upon the tablecloth or let it run out of his mouth. His son and his son's wife were disgusted at this, so the old grandfather at last had to sit in the corner behind the stove, and they gave him his food in an earthenware bowl, and not even enough of it. And he used to look towards the table with his eyes full of tears.
>
> Once, too, his trembling hands could not hold the bowl, and it fell to the ground and broke. The young wife scolded him, but he said nothing and only sighed. Then they brought him a wooden bowl for a few half-pence, out of which he had to eat.
>
> They were once sitting thus when the little grandson of four years old began to gather together some bits of wood upon the ground. 'What are you doing there?' asked the father. 'I'm making a little trough,' answered the child, 'for father and mother to eat out of behind the stove when I'm big.'
>
> The man and his wife looked at each other for a while, and presently began to cry. Then they took the old grandfather to the table, and henceforth always let him eat with them, and likewise said nothing if he did spill a little of anything.

This is the story that I use a lot in my sessions, and it never ceases to get the desired reaction of making people thing about their behaviour and how it impacts on others.

ONE OUR ACTIONS CAN HURT OTHERS.

And it can hurt others either intentionally or unintentionally.

A big part of our leadership training programs is about intention. I ask leaders what their intentions are. Are their intentions to help or hurt, to harm or heal? The majority of leaders have the right intent.

In the moment, when the pressure is on, or during a crisis event, things can change. And intent can change quickly. And your team might not be your priority in the moment.

It's in those moments that you could metaphorically 'put someone behind the stove.' Out of sight, out of mind! Or you could exclude them. Or put them in your out-group. Like the son and his wife did.

LEADER ACTION

The message is to be aware of your intent before you make people decisions or have courageous conversations.

TWO OUR ACTIONS CAN INFLUENCE OTHERS.

And it can influence others either intentionally or unintentionally.

Leading by example is not an important element of leadership; it's the only element of leadership. Your teams don't listen to you as much as they watch you. Your teams are continuously observing your behaviour for the signs and signals of how to behave.

They're looking for the minimum line of what's acceptable. And the maximum line of what's expected. So that they can stay within those lines and avoid falling below what's accepted, while aiming to perform above what's expected (exceeding expectations).

And you don't have to say anything to influence behaviour at times. You just have to act. Like the four-year-old grandson did.

LEADER ACTION

The message is to always behave in a way that's in alignment with your values. That's legal, moral, and ethical, and that has high integrity.

THREE OUR ACTIONS CAN SERVE OTHERS.

And it can serve others to see them succeed.

There are times when you might need to swallow your pride. Change your mind, change your decision. And that's OK. It's sometimes better to change your decision than to continue to argue or fight for an outcome that's not possible. Changing your decision is a sign of courage, not a lack of it, but most leaders don't see it that way. They see it as a sign of weakness or a lack of conviction, when the opposite is the case.

Being in service, even if it means implementing a change, or a changed decision, is important. You can be in service, like the son and his wife were.

LEADER ACTION

The message is to be aware of what your teams are experiencing, and what you might need to change to upgrade their experience.

Your behaviour matters. It can impact others—in their experience as a team member, and in how they behave as a leader. And this is particularly important when you're leading at the top of the corporate food chain, which is always going to be one of your biggest challenges.

LEADING LEADERS IS THE BIGGEST LEADERSHIP CHALLENGE

I went from leading a team to leading leaders. I'll never forget how hard that was. Really, really, hard. Here I was, leading great humans that lead their own teams, who have their own styles, leadership goals, and career goals. It was tough going, and I had to update, upgrade, and upskill my leadership skills. And Quickly.

Now that I work with CEOs and C-Suite teams, I still hear from senior leaders that their biggest leadership challenge is the leadership of other senior leaders. And I can relate.

So, what are the skills that are required to lead senior leaders? Read on to find out what my own experience is, and what over 700 1:1 coaching sessions has taught me about leading other leaders.

ONE MICROMANAGING DOESN'T WORK.

One of the most common issues that senior leaders have is that they're micromanaged. Yes, the CEO, sometimes knowing exactly what they're doing, chooses micromanaging as a strategy. And the C-Suite don't like it. They don't respond, and they don't buy in.

Micromanagement is where managers feel the need to control aspects of their team members work and decision making—to an extreme degree, more than is necessary or healthy for a usual working relationship. Many people will have experienced micromanagement and its impact at some point in their careers. As much as it might appear to be working, it doesn't.

For leaders who've climbed the ladder of corporate success, who are sitting in the C-Suite, they feel like they've got a handle on leadership. They feel like they're building a high-performing team, and they feel like they're absolutely capable of leading others and making decisions. Micromanagement just doesn't do it for them.

LEADER ACTION

CEO, give your leadership team the chance to shine, to decide, and to develop professionally.

TWO THE PERSONALITIES ARE BIGGER.

Senior leaders are more confident. They're more committed. They're more courageous. And they're bigger personalities. With big personalities come big opinions, and big ideas. Which takes a solid CEO who's capable of dealing with big personalities.

Yes, leading big personalities is a big job. CEOs with a range of big personalities on their senior leadership team need, above everything else, to take on the role of facilitator. That means to make sure that everyone on the senior leadership team has a voice, has a value, and has a vested interest in the team as an aligned unit.

CEOs who can facilitate have the ability to question, listen, and decide. They have the ability to engage everyone in conversation, and they have the ability to get all opinions prior to make a decision.

LEADER ACTION

CEO, give your leadership team the ability to contribute, to be heard, and to add value.

THREE THE SILOING GETS WORSE.

For me, the biggest challenge that I see CEOs having is that their senior leaders forget that they're also part of a team. The C-Suite can get focused on their own patch, their own department, their own business unit. Even when decisions impact other senior leaders and other departments. That's called building empires, or becoming siloed.

Siloing is a big issue in organisations, because it doesn't just occur at the most senior levels of the organisation. Issues with siloing flow down through the business, and team members at every level pick up on it. They know that the senior leaders aren't aligned, and it does nothing for morale, motivation, and making things happen.

Siloing stifles creativity. Siloing stifles cultures. Siloing stifles commitment. And siloing generally starts at the upper echelons of the organisation.

LEADER ACTION

CEO, encourage your leadership team to work together, talk together, and decide together.

Remember that role modelling leadership to leaders is about showing them how to be a good leader. A good leader isn't just a fair and suppportive boss; it's one who supports team members to grow and develop professionally, to contribute meaningfully to the team, and to work together seamlessly in achieving common goals.

Your job isn't just to support leadership roles; it's to create more leaders. Let your behaviour demonstrate that. Because people and their wellbeing should be your focus, always.

ACTIVITY 3.3
ROLE MODEL LEADERSHIP

Take some time now to think about what you've learnt in the last chapter.

The series of questions on the following pages will encourage you to think about what you can do to develop your capacity for strong leadership during crisis times, and ways you can effectively role model that leadership to others to positively influence both their work life, and their development.

How have you led your team through crisis events?

How predictable to your team do you think you are in your emotions, behaviour, and focus?

Can you detail times where your actions as a leader have hurt, influenced, or served your team members?

Answer honestly. Do you micromanage your team members?

How well do you lead leaders, especially ones with big personalities?

Answer honestly. As a leader, are you working in a silo, or are you fully integrated into the team?

Answer honestly. Do you condone bad behaviour in the workplace by walking past it?

Introspect honestly. Think of what your team members have seen and heard you do, and whether you can be proud of that or not.

SKILL IV
DEAL WITH DIFFICULTIES

TEAMS IN TURMOIL DON'T FUNCTION AS THEY SHOULD, DON'T COMMUNICATE WITH CARE, AND DON'T HAVE A PSYCHOLOGICALLY SAFE CULTURE.

In this book, I've covered situations where leaders want to make their high-performing team even higher performing. Most of my work is with these teams—the teams who are in good shape, and who are dedicated to trying to improve their performance.

But we still get some calls from leaders who are frustrated or struggling with a team in turmoil. A team that's not functioning as it should, team members who aren't communicating with care, and teams that don't have a psychologically safe culture.

Sadly, I've had a few of these conversations, and I can help the leader save some time on the phone with me. If I have a relationship with the leader, my first question is 'who's the person?', or 'who are the two people?' The reason that I ask one of those questions is that it's generally never more than one or two team members who are struggling to connect, but it still affects the whole team's dynamics.

If you've been following my posts, you'll know that 1) I'm a fairly simple writer (and human), and 2) I break team dynamics down to two things. Outputs and relationships. This is our high-performing team model. The outputs are what the team does. The stuff. The things. The KPIs, the measures, the outcomes, the production from the team. The relationships are how the team does what they do. How the team members work together. The communication, the connection, the care factor, and the psychological safety—or lack of it.

The main thing to consider is that most teams will tell me (when we do a survey) that their outputs are going well. They get their work done. A team in turmoil might even rate themselves as being high on outputs. The challenge is that outputs are at risk if relationships aren't strong. In my experience, a team in turmoil is just not able to sustain high output for a long period of time, when the team members struggle to work together—and struggle to deal with each other.

From a 'how to' perspective, if you have a high-performing team, focus on outputs because your relationships are in good shape and your team could work together to get more done (if they're not already at capacity). If you have a team in turmoil, it's time to really lean into the relationships in your team, and how to improve them.

But how do you do that? Glad you asked. Here are some thoughts, and three things you might consider.

ONE A TEAM CHARTER SESSION WILL REALLY HELP.

Team charters are a winner. But the message here really is don't try this at home (or alone) without a strong and capable facilitator. This could be a TGG facilitator (reach out) or someone from HR or from BI. Please, as the leader, if you have a team in turmoil, don't take this on yourself. You need to lead the session, not run it. Facilitating a team charter workshop with a team in turmoil is a learnt skill, and one that takes a significant amount of conversational control. And conversational management. Because, unfortunately, there will be conflict.

So what's a team charter? Glad you asked that question, too. A team charter is an overview of things like team beliefs, behaviours, or visions or values. Team charters help connect teams back to both purpose and people.

It's what we all commit to doing, and how we commit to being. How we'll treat each other. How we'll communicate. And what happens when we don't follow through on our commitments to treat each other with respect and high care factor. We don't have to be best friends with our teammates, but we do need to be able to work with them in a respectful way. If you'd like an enjoyable work life, that is. And don't want to work in a team in turmoil.

From experience, a team charter would be the best way to create alignment in a team that's not working together. Don't thank me now.

TWO LEADERSHIP CONVERSATIONS ALSO HELP.

One of the biggest issues with teams in turmoil (in my experience) is that the leader is avoiding the conversations that matter. The leader doesn't want to address the team members that are causing the challenges.

You see, what can happen is that the team member/s causing others grief can be the highest performers. These team members are high in the output section. The leader is afraid that if they take on the high performer, even when they're disrespecting others, the team member might drop off on performance, or might leave.

Remember this: you can't lead someone you need. Your highest performers don't have the right to hurt others, just because they're high performers. Leaders, have the conversation. It's not a performance conversation; it's a values-based conversation. It's a code of conduct conversation.

Also remember this: what you walk past, you condone. The more the leader ignores the behaviour, the more the team loses faith in their leader. Because the leader is not addressing the issue. And the team is still in turmoil. And yes, sometimes I get the job of talking to all team members to understand what's happening in the team. Which is cool, I can be unbiased—but at the end of the day, with or without the information I provide, the leader will have to have leadership conversations, and need to set behavioural boundaries.

THREE PAY ATTENTION TO TRIGGERS.

Understand the concept of triggers. And how both leader behaviour and team member behaviour causes unwanted and negative emotions to show up. And to show up in a way that drives poor behavioural response patterns. What I mean by triggers is those words or actions that cause team members to lose their cool. In other words, they lose their marbles, and say or do things are uncool.

If you're a leader, consider understanding more about Daniel Goleman's[6] work on triggers. One thing that's worth researching is his list of them. He identifies the top five negative emotional triggers in the workplace as the following:

- Condescension and lack of respect,
- Being treated unfairly,
- Being unappreciated,
- Feeling that you're not being listened to or heard, and
- Being held to unrealistic deadlines.

These areas tap straight into the Amygdala, and the limbic system—the structure in the brain that deals with fight, flight, or freeze—and thus is responsible for instant emotional reactions such as high levels of stress and panic. And anger.

As a leader, or even as a team member, these triggers are important to understand. The more you can avoid doing or saying something that would cause a team member to react badly, the smoother your team will run. Being consistently alert to them will go a long way in helping you deal with difficulties—including insidious problems like office politics.

WHAT THE ACTUAL...IS GOING ON WITH ALL THE OFFICE POLITICS HAPPENING RIGHT NOW?!

What is it with the amount of workplace politics that seem to be happening everywhere? Politics are hard to cope with at times. Until you understand what's really going on, that is.

Firstly though, this section was prompted by a trend that's showing up in my coaching conversations around how stressful office politics can be. And there really is a lack of understanding of why people form alliances or groups to increase their own personal or professional power. When you look at it from a psychological viewpoint, why wouldn't you play politics, if it helps you get ahead? Because it makes you look like a twit, that's why. And because it's not fair on the humans that can't understand why you favour some people and not others, and why some get the royal and special treatment, when others don't.

You usually only get to really understand office politics when you've made a decision that offends someone, who then rallies the posse in support of why it was such a bad decision. Or you might say something to someone who's aligned with someone else, or who's related to so and so, or who only spends the training budget on one team, so don't bother asking.

The two things about office politics are that they're generally not process related (they're people or power related), and they create a stressful working environment. It's hard to create conscious control when you're always on guard for what you might say that might get back to someone else, right? And it affects people's ability to advance their career and get ahead. Business News Daily notes that:

> Politics is bubbling over into nearly every aspect of our lives; and the office, it seems, is not immune. Research from Robert Half's Accountemps revealed that political discord plays a significant role in today's office life.
>
> Overall, 55% of employees say they partake at least somewhat in office politics, with most of those doing so to advance their careers. The study found that 76% of workers believe that

office politics affect their efforts to get ahead, an increase of
20% within four years.[14]

So, what can you do to deal with difficulties when you're working in a
political work environment?

ONE ACCEPT IT.

Reconcile within yourself that there are things and people outside of your
control (sorry if that's too blunt, or too boring, or too hard). There are some
things at work that we just can't change, things that we just have to live
with (or leave). Accept the fact, and understand that some people are just
political by nature (or nurture) and that they'll act like that, regardless of
what you say or think. Get your head around the fact that some people
are just not great at doing human stuff (see The Dark Triad by Paulhus &
Williams[11] for more information on the personality types that might be prone
to political kinds of behaviour).

TWO STAY IN CONTROL.

This should be self-explanatory, but with all the other pressures out there
right now, I'm hearing from coaching clients that politics is another stressor,
and sometimes the proverbial straw that breaks the camel's back. I get it.
It can be the thing that sets you off, especially when the politician thinks
they're putting one over you. Watch your self-talk and watch your emotional
state—it comes out in your behaviour, even if you don't think it does.

THREE WORK WITH IT.

And I mean that in the right way. If you can use the situation to your
advantage, without compromising your values and your dignity, go right
ahead. If you need to get a decision made, and you think the grapevine will
help you, go right ahead, I say. This point is not so much 'if you can't beat
them, join them' as it's 'anything that's done legally, morally, and ethically
can't go too wrong.' Remember to have the right intent. If you hurt others to
get your way, you're becoming complicit in the politics yourself.

FOUR OVER-COMMUNICATE.

If I had only two words to help you deal with office politics, these are the two
words I'd share with you: Over-communicate. Yes. Over-communicate (you

need to hear those two words seven times for it to sink apparently, or so the org psychs tell us). I won't write it seven times. Maybe read them seven times either quietly, or out aloud. If you read them aloud, and others ask, share this section with them, in case they're struggling too. But what does it mean to over-communicate? It means this—and I cannot emphasise how important this is, in case you haven't noticed—think before you act.

Ask yourself this question: who will be affected, or interested, or impacted, by what I'm about to do? The decision, or the action. Over-communicating means being ahead of important communication and decisions, so that you can ring the person first. Email them, to let them know what you're up to. When someone asks you to stop over-communicating, you'll know you're doing it right! Over-communicate. And you can use this strategy in general terms, if you want to, depending on your business, your leader, and your team. But please be in front of the game on any big decisions or actions. It'll help. (And I got it in seven times—yay!)

FIVE STAY CLEAR.

Yes, this is the hard one. Hard, not impossible. The more you can stay clear, the less you'll be embroiled in the tragedy and the impending catastrophe that can come from office politics. Or not. Some of the time, people (and leaders, sadly) get away with hurting others because they're—wait for it... you've heard these words before—a protected species. As well as over-communicating, please do whatever you can to remove yourself from any office politics going on around you.

These strategies are really important in dealing with the difficulty of office politics, and they're yet another reason why it's so important for you to have conscious control. With it, you'll become as adept at navigating office politics as you are at avoiding other minefields in the workplace—including the age-old issue of groupthink.

HOW TO AVOID GROUPTHINK, AND WHY YOU SHOULD

On 28 January 1986, NASA made the decision to launch *The Challenger*. That decision resulted in what's called to this day 'the Challenger disaster.'

What was the disaster? The Space Shuttle Challenger disaster was a fatal incident on January 28, 1986, in the United States space program where the space shuttle *Challenger* (OV-099) broke apart 73 seconds into its flight, killing all seven crew members aboard. (Credit: Wiki).

It's amazing when you read the story about the disaster and the review into what happened. The saddest part of the tragedy is that it could (and should) have been avoided. An engineer told his wife the night before the launch that it would blow up. And the part that failed, causing the explosion, was one (or two—depending on which website you read) O-ring, that wasn't rated for the cold temperatures that it was exposed to.

What does an O-ring cost? Not much. But what does it cost when leaders don't listen to their teams, when they have great ideas? In this case, the costs—human and financial—were significant, and tragic.

And, from all reports, there wasn't just one engineer, but four, that voiced their concerns about what could happen if NASA followed through with the *Challenger* launch that day—a day that was both colder than other launches, and too cold for the O-rings on the *Challenger*.

But the senior engineers (and the contractor engaged by NASA at the time) made the call to launch, even after having been told what might happen. After all, the US President was going to address the American people, to tell them how well it went, and how great America and NASA were at launching space craft into the thermosphere.

The investigation into the *Challenger* disaster coined the phrase 'groupthink', which means that the group has more power over the discussion (and the decision) than those (individuals) who might know better. Investopedia describes it this way:

> **Groupthink is a phenomenon that occurs when a group of individuals reaches a consensus without critical reasoning or evaluation of the consequences or alternatives. Groupthink is based on a common desire not to upset the balance of a group of people.**

In other words, groupthink doesn't consider all opinions. Some of which might be valid. Very valid, in the case of the *Challenger*.

So, just for a moment, put yourself in the position of the contractor or chief engineer in 1986, and ask yourself what you would have done. What decision would you have made? What would your priorities have been? Fame, fortune, and media exposure, or life preservation?

What's important, as we learn from tragedies like the *Challenger* disaster, is thinking about how they can apply to our situations. Most of the time we aren't responsible for the lives of seven humans, but at the same time, we have responsible decisions to make.

Here's how to avoid groupthink.

ONE TAKE A PRIORITY AWARENESS APPROACH.

Decision making is a key requirement of leaders. Especially leaders under pressure, when they might not have all the information, or they need to decide quickly. When the human brain is in decision-making mode, all that's happening is that it's processing possibilities based on priority propositions.

That means that all decisions are priority based. What your priority is in the moment will ultimately determine how you make the decision. Let's take safety for a moment, because that's the easiest was to describe this topic (and it relates to the *Challenger* disaster). Are you focused on the safety of humans, or are you focused on production, or some other priority that you probably shouldn't be focused on in the moment?

This paragraph could be called 'be aware of your values', as most of the time, our priorities in the moment of decision making are a subset of our values. The way to be aware of your priorities is to be very clear, and very aware of the rationale for your decision—and to be able to explain that clearly.

LEADER ACTION

If you feel like you're trying to convince yourself or others with words like 'the risk is worth the reward', or 'we should get away with it', rethink your priorities and rethink your decision. Then, when you're aware of your priorities, share them, and ask for feedback or input to ensure that others get the chance to contribute. Don't let your priorities drive a groupthink mindset for the team that's making critical decisions.

TWO HAVE A DEFERENCE TO EXPERTISE APPROACH.

As part of the review of the *Challenger* disaster, and a range of other major catastrophic events, the term 'High Reliability Organisation' (HRO) was coined. HRO theory flowed out of Normal Accident Theory, which led a group of researchers at the University of California, Berkeley (Todd LaPorte, Gene Rochlin, and Karlene Roberts)[8] to study how organisations working with complex and hazardous systems operated error free. And how events like the *Challenger* disaster could have been avoided, and how similar high-risk organisations did avoid those types of tragedies.

At the core of a HRO, there are five key principles, which are essential for any improvement initiative to succeed: deference to expertise, reluctance to simplify, sensitivity to operations, commitment to resilience, and preoccupation with failure.

Although all these principles are super important, the most important principle is the deference to expertise. What that means is to defer to the person who has the most expertise to make the decision. Or defer to the group of people who have the most expertise to make the decision. In the case of the *Challenger* disaster, there were four engineers who all came to the same conclusion about the O-ring temperature rating, but none of their opinions were considered (they were ignored) when it came to deciding to launch the *Challenger*.

And it doesn't matter how low you go in the organisation to defer to expertise. If it's a junior person that you need to involve in the decision, so be it. If they have the information that could help, or that could save a life, leaders are obliged to consider their input.

LEADER ACTION

Deferring to expertise is the quickest and easiest way to prevent groupthink, because you overtly and openly encourage input from the right people. If you're prepared to listen to that input, you'll notice how much value is added to the decision-making process.

These strategies aren't just effective in avoiding groupthink. They're strategies that uplift your team members, by giving them a voice and inviting them to use their valuable skills in dealing with difficulties. Commit to the strategies of uplifting your team—and you might never have to hear some of the worrying things that team members say to their leaders.

THE 5 THINGS LEADERS NEVER WANT TO HEAR FROM THEIR TEAMS

I've had some great leaders. One of my favourite leaders of all time is a person called Pat (let's use that name—it happens to be their real name). Pat was the human that shared with me the power of languaging, and how to listen to what people are really saying. Pat shared that sometimes it's blatantly obvious, and at other times, not so much. Pat's coaching is some of the reason that we now focus so much on languaging as part of our leadership workshops and training. In relation to the blatant comments that team members make, there are some that should move you to action, Pat explained. And they really are things you don't want to hear from you team.

Here's some of the big (and worrying) things that team members say to their leaders.

ONE I DON'T FEEL VALUED.

This is a tough one, and it goes straight to the solar plexus. If you follow any of my work at all, you'll understand how importantly I take the word value/s. Our values drive our behaviour, and one of our greatest human needs is to feel valued. Particularly by our leader.

What feeling valued is all about is feeling heard. This section could be 'I don't feel heard', but not feeling valued is a more common statement made by team members who don't feel like they have a voice.

Feeling valued is related to the psychological safety aspect of leadership, and it's about making it safe for team members to both contribute (with ideas or opinions) and to challenge the norms (being creative and innovative). Leaders that lead with low psychological safety will end up with team members that don't feel valued, because they don't feel like what they say ever matters.

LEADER ACTION

When you're with your team, either 1:1 or in a group setting, please be present. Be focused. Be a listener. Listen with an open heart and an open mind. You might not like what you hear, but it helps your team members feel valued if you're able to hold the space and listen to their ideas and concerns without judgement.

TWO I DON'T FEEL CARED FOR.

This is another tough one. It's not as common as the first one, but it happens, and leaders hear it (or team members tell it to other team members, and the leader might not even know). Being cared for is another human need, and one that, when violated, has an adverse impact on the team member. Who might check out or give up.

Feeling cared for is related to the psychological connection aspect of leadership, and it's about making time for team members. Yes, making time. Scheduling time with team members (both 1:1 and as a team) is a critical element of leadership, and when that's ignored or forgotten, your team feel like their leader doesn't care. Team members might say that they're not a priority for their leader, or that their leader is too busy for them. Ouch.

LEADER ACTION

Jump into your calendar and schedule 1:1 meetings with your team

THREE I DON'T FEEL SUPPORTED.

This is an interesting one, that can relate to a range of issues. The main area is in career progression—for the team member who has big ambitions, this is really important. And it's tough for the leader team member dynamic when there's a misalignment on career progression and pathways.

The other situations that might leave a team member feeling unsupported are during times of big projects or big decisions. With big projects or big decisions, team members need some level of direction. Yes, it might be minimal. But direction is important. I work with leaders at all levels of organisational charts, and they all need direction from their leaders—and they all struggle without it.

In our coaching sessions, I always ask our coachees if they feel like they have their leader's support. Most of the time it's a yes, but at times it's a no. And in these situations, my coaching is to not go out on a limb too far when making a decision, or taking an action, in case the branch breaks. Without leader support, team members can become very isolated very quickly, and can overstep boundaries or levels of responsibility. For more guidance on this one, see the book Radical Candor by Kim Scott,[12] where she talks about the balance between caring and direction.

LEADER ACTION

If a team member doesn't feel like you support their career, have a career conversation to help you get clearer on how you can support them. If it's a big project or big decision, don't say 'I'll let you decide.' If they ask for guidance, please give it to them, as best as you can.

FOUR I DON'T FEEL LIKE I MAKE A DIFFERENCE.

This is more sad than anything. It's another statement around human needs not being met. We all want to feel like our work matters to someone, particularly our leaders and our organisation.

Feeling like we make a difference is related to the psychological empowerment aspects of leadership, where team members feel like their work makes an impact and has a level of meaning. I know I've felt like this in the past, in some roles, where I questioned how much of a difference I was making to the team or the business. It's hard to show up each day when we feel like we don't really matter, and when we feel like no one would notice if we weren't there.

LEADER ACTION

If a team member doesn't feel like they're making a difference, it's important to find out why, and consider how that can be addressed. There might be an explanation around why the team member's work matters, or why it's valued.

FIVE I DON'T FEEL EMPOWERED.

This is perhaps the easiest of the big five listed here to deal with as a leader. Feeling unempowered means not feeling like you have the right level of responsibility. Not being trusted. Or not given adequate decision-making ability. Sometimes, this statement can relate to not feeling fully utilised in the role. The team member might be saying that they've got more to offer.

Feeling empowered is also related to the psychological empowerment aspects of leadership (competence and self-determination), and it's related to team members feeling like they're hamstrung in their role, and that they can't act without the direction of their leader, instead of being trusted by their leader to make decisions that relate to their role. A lack of empowerment can be the result of very transactional leadership styles.

LEADER ACTION

If a team member doesn't feel empowered, this is a sign they feel like you don't trust them to step up and make the decisions that they need to make. And that might be the case, so work out how you can develop more trust in that team member, or how you can give them more decision-making responsibility.

Think about which one of these is most important to you, which one you might have heard from a team member, and what you can do about it. It'll help give you perspective on how to move forward and effectively deal with difficulties with team members, as well as difficulties with other leaders— like leaders who go BOOM when things go BOOM.

DEALING WITH YOUR LEADER WHO GOES BOOM WHEN THINGS GO BOOM

Leaders seem to be going BOOM more often. Or at least that's what our coaching clients are telling us. We're hearing a lot of 'when the pressure comes on, my leader loses it.'

So, how do we coach our clients to deal with a leader who can't create conscious control? Let's unpack.

THE OUT-OF-CONTROL LEADER

Firstly, we need to understand what's going on for the leader who goes BOOM when things around them go BOOM. And there are both reasons and rationales, but they are in no way excuses for their behaviour.

Some leaders, as young or as old as they are, have never made the effort or taken the time to learn the skills of conscious control (aka: emotional and behavioural control).

Some leaders are born (or bred) in a way that predisposes them to going BOOM. For more information on personality traits like narcissism (a little overused these days, but a relevant term), see The Dark Triad by Paulhus & Williams[11] and see if your leader's behaviour is listed there.

Finally, some leaders just don't care how they impact other humans. I've worked for one of these, and they don't change their style easily. And no amount of feedback will change them.

BOUNDARIES ARE IMPORTANT

You need to have very clear boundaries relating to how you'll allow yourself to be treated by your leader, and you need to share those boundaries with your leader. Either when they go BOOM (hard), or when things are quiet and you can create the expectation (easier, but not easy). Without boundaries, you're not being clear on what you will or won't tolerate, and you won't be able to communicate those.

CREATE CONSCIOUS CONTROL

The most common reaction I hear from our leadership coaching clients is that when their leader goes BOOM, so do they. It's like 'if you can shout at me, I can shout at you.' Which is uncool. Sorry. I know your leader has gone

BOOM, but it doesn't help to react in kind (which is a natural reaction, by the way). It takes conscious control not to react like that. The trick with conscious control is to respond not react. Use your frontal lobes (smart), not your limbic (emotional) brain.

ALWAYS DEBRIEF THE BOOM

If your leader goes BOOM—and most people don't do this one, because they're just happy it's over, but you must, it's critical!—debrief.

After a BOOM event, things will settle down. When they do, it's time to unpack what happened, and ask for a commitment that you won't be treated like that again. And get that commitment.

CHANGE ROLES OR LEADERS

Don't threaten to leave. That's never a good look. Just do it (like Nike)! Just move out of the team or the organisation and leave with integrity. Share at your exit interview why you've left, and the fact that you've been hurt once too many times. You never know what change it might effect.

But dealing with difficulties isn't just about dealing with difficult people. You cause difficulties too, albeit unintentionally—difficulties like committing the cardinal sin of leadership.

HOW TO NOT COMMIT THE CARDINAL SIN OF LEADERSHIP

The cardinal sin of leadership is not doing one-on-ones (1:1) with your team members. Even worse than that is scheduling those meetings every week, fortnight, or month, and either not attending them, or continually rescheduling. These behaviours are very damaging to the relationship between the leader and team member.

There's only one thing worse than either not scheduling, or rescheduling, those meetings—and that's to use the excuse that you're just too busy. Any leaders out there that say they're too busy for their team are just saying that their team member (and connecting with them regularly) is not a priority for the leader. 'I'm too busy' is translated (subconsciously, by the team member) as 'my leader has higher priorities than our relationship.' Which is uncool.

And the reality is that leaders are busy. They have too much to do. They're stretched, and for some, taking the time to have the regular 1:1s that they need to can be a real challenge for their time and their calendar.

Here are some real practical tips and tricks to help you stay committed

and focused on your one-on-ones.

ONE KNOW HOW IMPORTANT THOSE MEETINGS ARE.

1:1 meetings are highly valued by team members. Sometimes, a 1:1 meeting is the only quality time that a team member gets with their leader. Most team members prepare well of these meetings, have a list of things to discuss with their leader, and generally make great use of the time. Obviously, some team members don't take them that seriously, but the message is that 1:1 meetings give employees face-to-face time to discuss the things that are important to them.

During COVID, Microsoft surveyed their leaders and teams to understand how important 1:1 meetings really are, and if the business benefits from them as much as the employee does. Their findings were published in a blog post titled The New Manager 1:1: Nurturing Employee Resiliency During Disruption and Change.

In short, and to unpack just how important 1:1 meetings are for a leader and team member, these meetings actually lead to less meetings overall. Winner. They lead to better collaboration and less work hours for team members. Winner. They lead to more resilient team members. And they lead to a better work life balance for team members, because the meetings are not just work related. Winner. The data is conclusive, and it demonstrates that if 1:1 meetings work during a high-stress time like during a global pandemic, imagine how well they'll work in your business now, all these years later.

And sometimes just knowing and acknowledging how important things are—like 1:1 meetings—can mean that you put higher priority on them, and don't reschedule or miss them.

TWO TAKE OWNERSHIP AND RESPONSIBILITY FOR YOUR CALENDAR.

This means not changing or rescheduling 1:1 meetings. It's hard to put it any other way, sorry.

I was going to leave this paragraph there, but that would be uncool, because I know that there are things that pop up that need your urgent attention. I get that, but I also get how your team members feel when they're 'rescheduled.' The big thing here is to have the conversation firstly about what else is happening that's preventing you from attending the 1:1 meeting. And it's not just being too busy. And if you do reschedule, make sure you attend the rescheduled meeting (and yes, you won't believe how many leaders I know that are in a perpetual cycle of rescheduling).

Also, if you have someone that coordinates your calendar, like I do, ask them to hold you accountable. Asking for their commitment also helps you to hold yourself accountable.

Also consider the use of notifications or other push prompts, to make sure you're in your office, or the meeting room, when your next 1:1 meeting is due to begin. At Microsoft, tools like MyAnalytics have manager-focused features that remind managers to maintain 1:1 connection with employees through nudges. If it's good enough for Microsoft, it should be certainly be good enough for us.

THREE KNOW THAT IT'S NEVER TOO LATE TO START.

Again, from the Microsoft study, When manager 1:1s hadn't been a long-term habit, increasing them had an immediate benefit. An IMMEDIATE benefit.

Imagine, as you sit and read this section, what else there is at your disposal that you could implement right now without much effort. And that'll help you create happier, more resilient, and better-balanced team members. If you can think of something, please feel free to send it to me, and I'll study it and write a post or book sections about it in the future.

Also in the future, we can unpack how to have great 1:1 meetings. Some leaders take the entire meeting, and give directions. Or in the last five minutes, ask 'and how are you going?' This is not optimal. But that's a conversation for another day.

I just can't think of anything else that's as good as 1:1 meetings for changing the dynamics in your team. They're extremely important. They create engaged team members and teams. They allow the leader to focus on building the relationship. And in my humble opinion, to reschedule or to not value 1:1 meetings is THE cardinal sin of leadership.

Dealing with difficulties is extremely important. But rather than just focusing on putting out fires, it's important to implement strategies before they're needed—strategies that underpin effective working relationships.

LEADERSHIP TEAMS NEED THIS ONE THING TO BE EFFECTIVE

Teams need not only strong leaders, but strong leadership teams. Senior leadership teams set the tone for the business, for the culture, for the vision, and for the strategic direction.

Every day, or every week, I get asked by a leader or a team member why their leadership team isn't aligned, why they're not singing the same tune, why they're not all focused on the same things. Generally, the problem is that the senior leadership team don't know that they're not aligned. And without alignment, it's only a matter of time before there are staff issues relating to psychological or physical safety.

In my experience of coaching a large number of senior leadership teams, alignment is the big thing that's missing in less effective Senior Leadership Teams (SLTs).

Here's how you increase it with your SLT.

ONE SENIOR LEADERS NEED BELIEF ALIGNMENT.

When we do SLT workshops, to help senior leadership teams to come together in a unified way, the first thing we work through is belief systems and belief alignment. This is a crucial part of the alignment process, because our beliefs drive our behaviour in an unconscious way. They drive our languaging, they drive our decisions, they drive our team leadership.

And they're deep down in our unconscious mind. They come from our conditioning, from our nurturing, and from our environment as we've gone through life. We are a sum of our experiences, and those experiences shape how we lead.

If senior leaders have different belief systems, and that shows up as different leadership behaviours, the teams will see and feel the misalignment.

LEADER ACTION

Take the time to align your belief systems. Start with what behaviours those beliefs should be driving.

TWO SENIOR LEADERS NEED VALUE ALIGNMENT.

The next part of our SLT workshops involves a personal value process. Our values drive our behaviour in a conscious way. If you asked someone to describe you, they'd use values-based words, like honest, happy, committed, motivated, or something similar.

Our values are those parts of our psyche that we call on when we need to make big decisions. Like investment decisions or people decisions. We lean into our integrity, or our respect, or our caring values.

We all have personal values. But so do organisations and leaders, and they need to align with the values of the organisation.

This is very, very, very important. Please don't underestimate how important it is for the SLT members to align their own values with each other, and with the values of the organisation. When senior leaders leave, they usually cite misaligned values as their reason for leaving.

The values need to be on the wall, visible. With bullet points of required behaviours under each value. SLTs need to lean into those values when they're making big decisions, and clearly explaining why they've been made.

LEADER ACTION

Take the time to get clear on your own values, then share them with the other senior leaders, and align those with the values of the business.

THREE SENIOR LEADERS NEED CULTURE ALIGNMENT.

The good news is that this one can take care of itself if the first two have been done properly. But even if they have, there's still a requirement for every SLT to be clear on what type of culture they're trying to drive in the business. Culture starts with the SLT.

Indeed.com writes:

> Organisational culture refers to a company's mission, objectives, expectations, and vision that guide its employees. Businesses with a strong organisational culture tend to be more successful than less structured companies because they have systems in place that promote employee performance, productivity and engagement.

In short, strong culture drives the desired behaviour at all levels of the organisation. When the senior leaders behave in a certain way, the whole business will follow suit. SLT members need to lead by example. Not leading by example is the quickest way to impact organisational culture.

LEADER ACTION

SLT members need to be aware of the impact of their behaviour on the teams. Lead by example is the key message here.

The process of dealing with difficulties doesn't always have to be reactive. Create a more aligned—and therefore, more effective—SLT, and far it goes towards creating a high-functioning, problem-free team.

ACTIVITY 3.4
DEAL WITH DIFFICULTIES

Take some time now to think about what you've learnt in the last chapter.

The series of questions on the following pages will encourage you to think about what you can do to help your team members when they're in turmoil, and to apply the lessons you've just learnt about dealing with difficulties in the process of uplifting your team.

Alternatively, spend some time just sitting and writing about how you've managed your team through crises in the past, and what skills you need to improve to overcome difficulties you're currently experiencing or are likely to experience in the future.

Do you have a team in turmoil? Can you think of skills you need to effectively lead them through their challenges?

Do you use a team charter? Why, or why not?

Do you think your team members showing or experiencing condescension or lack of respect in the workplace? If so, how can you address it?

Answer honestly. Do you think your team members feel they are being treated unfairly, or not being unappreciated?

How can you better help your team members to feel like they're being listened to—and heard?

Answer honestly. Do you believe you set realistic deadlines, or are you expecting too much from your team members?

Do you think there are unhealthy office politics happening in your workplace right now? If so, how can you better manage it?

What are your highest priorities in the workplace? Are you focused on the safety of humans, or are you focused on production, or some other priority?

Do you defer to team members with deeper knowledge and superior expertise? Why, or why not?

Answer honestly. Do you commit the cardinal sin of leadership?

SKILL V
DEMONSTRATE RADICAL CANDOUR

SOME LEADERS REALLY STRUGGLE WHEN THEY'RE CHALLENGED BY THEIR TEAM MEMBERS.

Even if the challenge is just an idea or an opinion, and one that shouldn't warrant an emotional reaction.

It's difficult, especially for leaders under pressure, to keep it together when everyone's got an idea on what could be improved. Or on how the team should be run. But it's OK for your team to offer suggestions.

It's better than OK. It's a great thing that team members want to offer suggestions and have input into the team's functioning, because it means they care about their work. That needs to be tempered of course, because every new idea won't fly. But it's about giving team members a voice. Remember that if team members aren't heard, they're hurt.

But what's radical candour? And what has it got to do with team members having a voice?

Radical candour was coined by Amy Edmondson as part of her research into how to create psychologically safe teams. Psychological safety was defined by Edmondson as a team or workplace culture where it's OK for team members 'to take interpersonal risks', without the fear of rejection, resentment or ridicule. Taking interpersonal risks is another way of saying 'speaking up without fear.'[4]

Radical candour is a leadership approach that doesn't only make it OK for people to share ideas and information, but actually encourages it.

In relation to leading with radical candour, there are three things to discourage in your team discussions, and there are three things to encourage. Let's start with the discourage first. Because these are the behaviours that will reduce psychological safety in your team.

When your team is sharing information, lean away from:

- **Ruinous Empathy**: insincerity in your responses, feedback, or praises, particularly the sugar-coating of criticism, so the other person doesn't feel bad (this comes from a place of caring);

- **Manipulative Insincerity**: insincerity in your responses, feedback or praises, without the sugarcoating, that's delivered with the wrong intent—to hurt or harm (this definitely doesn't come from a place of caring); and

- **Obnoxious Aggression**: this is about being clear, and not kind (some people call it brutal honesty), and unlike manipulative insincerity, it's not meant to hurt, but it does, due to the message's poor delivery.

When your team is sharing information, lean into:

- **Promoting Respect**: we don't have to agree, but we do need to respect each other;

- **Welcoming Curiosity**: even team members with ideas might not have all the information required—encourage them to ask questions as much as they provide answers; and

- **Acknowledging Ideas**: all ideas are relevant, when they're shared. It's not until they're discussed that they can be discarded (might be a short discussion, or a long one). And, if they don't fly, share why; and if they were the wrong idea, share the mistake.

If you can lean into these three leadership behaviours, you'll create a psychologically safe team, you'll be leading with radical candour, and you'll encourage your team to share and contribute ideas and opinions in a safe environment. You'll also be prepared to be challenged, in good ways.

HOW TO MAKE CHALLENGER SAFETY A THING IN YOUR TEAM

In the book The Four Stages of Psychological Safety, Timothy R Clark[2] unpacks how to develop a team that feels safe to challenge the norms. Challenger safety is the fourth and final rung on the ladder (with inclusion safety, learner safety, and contributor safety being the first three).

Inclusion safety is about how well the team includes and integrates outsiders into the team. Learner safety is how much growth, development and learning are encouraged and adopted. Contributor safety relates to how safe people feel to contribute and to do their best work. And challenger safety is about how safe team members feel to speak up, and how safe they feel to offer ideas, opinions, and views. And to be creative and innovative. To think outside the box. To try new things. Without the fear of resentment, ridicule, or rejection.

So, how does a leader achieve that in their team?

ONE MAKE IT EXPECTED.

This is an important first step. Leaders need to be able to state clearly that they would like to be challenged, and need to hold the expectation that their team should feel safe to come up with creative solutions to problems. Leader languaging should be around expecting input and expecting their team to challenge the norms.

Creating the expectation of input is providing a license to innovate. That license might include incremental innovation, or it might be innovation at a disruption level. It might take the Google approach that gives team members thinking time as part of their work, to come up with great ideas, and then to present them. Gmail is one idea that came from thinking time, and Google being willing to be challenged on their business norms.

TWO MAKE IT ACCEPTABLE.

I get that this one seems redundant given that as a leader, you've made challenger safety an expectation. But here's the challenge for leaders, as I hear during coaching sessions: team members that have a license to innovate take that license and innovate. They do come up with ideas. They do challenge the norms, and they do offer solutions to problems that may not have been thought of previously.

And that can be tough for a leader. Leaders can be inundated with improvement ideas. This really can be overwhelming. Seriously. At some stage during the development of challenger safety, leaders think that 'you need to be careful what you ask for.' Which is cool. It means your team is committed, not just interested, and they feel safe enough to be part of the future growth of the team.

The way to think about this one is to consider the Tuckman model of team development, from forming to storming to norming to performing. Here's the thing about that model—it shows that during the storming stage, the team culture deteriorates (drops) for a period, until the team can come out the other side, and make challenger safety the norm (Google that model, if you're not aware of it). What it's really saying is that during the storming phase, there are issues at a team level, due to everyone wanting to raise their ideas and opinions. This stage should be called brainstorming because that's what it is. It's a phase where leaders need to have an open mind and an open heart.

And leaders need to not react with negative emotions when they're overwhelmed with the ideas and opinions offered by their team. This is where emotional intelligence comes into it.

THREE MAKE IT RADICAL.

Making challenger safety real is to do it with radical candour (from the book of the same name by Kim Scott[12]). In that book, Scott unpacks the most important thing about psychological safety, and that's about having conversations with radical candour. Which means challenging directly, but challenging with high care factor.

For the leader, the biggest challenge with challenger safety is sharing with team members that some ideas won't fly, and why. This is an important part of the challenge safety process, as there will be ideas that aren't right for the team or that just aren't right at that particular time. It's how these conversations are handled that will determine whether the team members continue to challenge or if they go into an 'it's all too hard to say anything' mode. If these conversations aren't handled well, it'll feel like rejection, ridicule or resentment.

The opposite of radical candour is manipulative insincerity. That is, to not challenge and to not care about the team member. These conversations have a lack of sincerity and a lack of specificity about them, and the team member leaves the conversation with more questions than answers about their idea or opinion. This happens when a leader beats around the bush when sharing that the idea or innovation isn't or won't be implemented for whatever reason.

FOUR TAKE A SUNSET-FIRST APPROACH.

What's the sunset-first approach? It's when you let the sun set on a major decision or the execution of a major decision. And you come back to the decision the next morning and make it then, after some thinking time (and maybe sleeping time).

I'm hearing you—when you're under pressure, this isn't always possible, or achievable. The decision must be made right now, or action must be taken right now. Or does it?

The issue with taking a right-now approach, as opposed to a sunset-first approach, is that you rush into making decisions. Or you're more worried about what your leader, or someone else, will think about the decision. I've been in senior leadership roles where plant downtime equates to millions of lost production, in both tonnes and dollars. But a sunset-first approach is still the right one when it comes to making major decisions. When you can.

And it demonstrates to your team that you're willing to wait for the right information, or the right people, or the right time, to make a big decision. Explain to others why you're willing to wait until tomorrow, then make the decision in the morning.

LEADER ACTION

If you don't do any of these, just listen to people that have some value to add to the decision. Don't let groupthink affect your decision making, especially when the consequences are high.

Sometimes, things need to be changed, which means you need to be challenged. Being a good leader means giving team members a chance to contribute to good change, and making it feel safe for them to do that. The new ideas support the business—and the space to challenge goes a long way towards creating a workplace that's psychologically safe.

WHY A SAFE SPACE IS MORE THAN PSYCHOLOGICAL SAFETY

Amy Edmondson[5] called it psychological safety. Simon Sinek[13] called it a circle of safety. We call it a safe space. Same, but different.

In our leading under pressure model, and with the support of research relating to how important it is to give your team members a voice, I'm going to say that a safe space is part of psychological safety. But it's way more than that.

To create a safe space, leaders need firstly to stay in control. It takes only one moment of out-of-control emotions to destroy years of creating trust and credibility as a leader. It takes leaders caring for their teams, not because they're told to, but because they want to. And it takes courage to make the decisions that might be unpopular, but that are made with the right intent. And of course, psychological safety is part of that. But, again, there's more to it.

Recently, I had a meeting with a business based in the USA. The leader of a 20-person team, in a 14,000-person business, explained what he'd managed to create in his team. And it was more than just giving his team a voice, and the ability to share ideas freely. It was deeper than that. It was about the way they communicated with each other. It was the intent of the communication, and it was about how their communication impacted others.

We discussed the fact that he had created a psychologically safe team. But we took the discussion further than that, and unpacked what really happens in his team to help everyone feel safe.

There were organisational things that business did, like unlimited sick leave and the flexibility of working from home. But it was more about the leader, and his team, and what they all did to foster a safe space. Remember, it's a team effort. Because a safe space is all about communication, and how we interact with other humans.

Here are the key elements of safe space communication. Firstly, have the right intent. That's a given. DO NO HARM. Don't hurt each other. Help not hurt; heal, not harm.

Then, give your team members permission to do the following.

ONE SPEAK WITH INFLUENCE.

Part of influence is interpreting the situation. Interpreting the position of the other human and acting accordingly. Influence can't happen without engagement and information. Information sharing, in a productive way, is influence. And it's not about winning a conversation, it's about influencing someone to share, to feel safe, and to act safe. It's listening to understand and not to respond, and being caring through your wording. Speaking with influence is about communicating with passion.

TWO SPEAK WITH IMPACT.

Be honest. Have real conversations. Be robust, with the right intent. Be memorable. Be the person that thinks fast and talks slow. Let silence do the heavy lifting. Be present. Be focused on the other human, and when the conversation is finished, hope that they share what a positive experience it was. Even if you had a tough conversation. Speaking with impact is about communicating on purpose.

THREE SPEAK WITH INSPIRATION.

Firstly, make commitments and keep them. Ask for help. Ask for a favour. Craft your call to action. Let people know why you're asking them to come on the journey (humans are quite simple creatures, a lot of the time, they just want to know why). Never leave the site of a meaningful conversation without the accompanying action, and someone to take responsibility for it.

Psychological safety is about being able to speak up. You create it with radical candour, and with conscious control, care factor, and courage. In giving people a voice to speak with ideas, and giving them permission to speak with influence, impact and inspiration, results in psychologically safe workplaces—and teams.

WHAT PINK CAN TEACH US ABOUT TEAM SAFETY

A few years ago, Mrs G and I were lucky enough to go to a Pink concert (*Beautiful Trauma Tour*). She was amazing. Then recently we sat down and watched the doco (*All I Know So Far*) about that tour, and we watched an amazing mum, an amazing wife, an amazing performer...and an amazing leader! I'm even more of a Pink fan now.

Here's why. Pink was so open with her behind-the-scenes shares. There were no holds barred, there were nappy changes (Jameson, who was a character, took a lot of Pink's attention). And of course, husband Carey Hart was always on hand, to be the parental support that a touring performer needs. There were hotels, concerts, daughter Willow conversations, tears and smiles, anguish and excitement. If you haven't watched the doco, don't thank me now. You'll love it, especially if you're a leader.

Here are some pearls of wisdom from Pink.

I DON'T GO OUT THE DOOR TO WORK—MY WORK AND MY HOME LIFE ARE THE SAME THING—OUR FAMILY GOES EVERYWHERE TOGETHER.

And not once did Pink say to her children that 'sorry Willow or Jameson, I have to work.' It was amazing to see her master the balancing act of performing and parenting.

There really wasn't a separation between the two areas of Pink's life, and she explained that, as parents, her and Carey worried that the kids might not be getting a conventional upbringing. Then, it was—'but hey, look at the life experiences they're getting.'

Although there were moments of emotional turmoil during the doco, the calmness that Pink demonstrated during the whole process of filming was something to be marvelled at. Whether she was performing or parenting, Pink has this ability to remain in control. It was an example of both leadership and parenting under pressure. Nothing seemed to really phase Pink (other than one stage change that she demanded...nicely).

I DON'T GET WHY OTHER PERFORMERS ARE ALWAYS AUDITIONING NEW PERFORMERS—OUR TEAM HAVE BEEN TOGETHER FOR TEN YEARS PLUS—WE LOVE OUR TEAM.

Pink just couldn't grasp why you'd want to change your team members, just because. Her philosophy was that loyal team members should be rewarded and recognised for their contribution.

They should enjoy their work. And that their leader's role is to encourage that. The tour was hard work, but at the same time, they were rewarded with a lot of downtime, and team members got the chance to socialise and have fun with Pink and her family.

There was a feeling of family to the tour, and to the team's interactions with Pink, Carey, Willow, and Jameson. It was lovely to watch how the team interacted with the children, and the team were not 'subordinates', but were active members of the decision-making process and the relevant conversations about the tour.

Pink used the word leadership on a few occasions. When she used that word, it was really about everyone, about being inclusive, and about being caring and conversational. Pink attended one of the team's birthday dinners while on tour—she sat at the table and cheered a team member on for their birthday. A little thing, but very symbolic.

YOUR TEAM HAS TO FEEL SAFE—SAFE TO SHOW UP, AND SAFE TO BE THE BEST VERSION OF THEMSELVES.

My jaw dropped. Go Pink. Talking about psychological safety (sort of). And it was just an off-handed comment that most people wouldn't have heard. But it's critical to what Pink believes and how she behaves. Pink encourages contribution. She shared openly that her leadership strategy is to encourage people to shine.

To encourage team members to share ideas. To encourage team members to grow. To encourage team members to learn and to become more during the touring process.

One comment Pink made was around hiring people smarter than her! How good is that? Pink—super star, world renowned, crazy good at what she does (and the only person that does the type of acrobatics that she does on stage)—talking in a documentary about team member safety. Wow.

Let's summarise what team safety means to Pink, from my understanding of the doco. Pink manages her emotional states and doesn't get flustered (she did when she got pulled off stage by a rope that wasn't connected properly—oops—but even angry, she kept it together well). She had care factor for her team and went out of her way to show that she cared. And they cared back. And she made courageous decisions like trusting her team to step up. Asking for input. And hiring people smarter than her.

This documentary is a leadership training program, really. And it's an example of a human who is as vulnerable as everyone else, but who also doesn't hurt people along the way. Pink's radical candour makes her the leader that everyone wants to work for—and you can be that leader, too.

Use radical candour, but not just to avoid hurting and harming. Use it to move your leadership further along the spectrum towards transformational—by learning how to show others you care about their wellbeing.

FROM 'I CARE' TO 'I REALLY KNOW HOW TO SHOW THAT I DO'

Most of the industries we work with have male leaders. And some have been in their roles for a long time. It's changing, slowly, which is positive. Our focus has always been to deliver programs that train and coach 'soft stuff for hard blokes', and that train leaders in general terms about how to better care for their teams.

Bob was one such leader. And for Bob it wasn't that he didn't care, it was that his team didn't feel like he did. And if teams don't feel cared for, they won't care for their leader, or their team. What you give out you get back—isn't that right?

So, what did Bob need to do to demonstrate care factor?

ONE BE PRESENT.

If you asked Bob's team, he was a powerhouse. He was always moving somewhere or doing something. Bob was energetic. He was passionate. His team thought that he was a strong leader, but they didn't think they were really on the top of his priority list. The work was. And the next catastrophe was Bob's focus.

This was really apparent when Bob's team really needed his attention. For example, when they had to discuss personal issues, Bob cared (and wanted to help) but didn't know how to show that.

Leaders who can't slow down and take their time to listen and support their teams when they need it aren't demonstrating care factor.

Bob's mission was to stop what he was doing. Sit still. Look at his team member. And listen. And be present. Have a conversation. And take the time to understand what's happening in their life that they need to talk about.

TWO LEARN TO SAY 'I CARE'.

Now this one shocked Bob. 'So, you're saying I should just tell people that I care about them?' he asked. Yes, Bob. Tell people, in whatever words feel right for you, that you care about them.

It's strange that telling team members that we care for them is such a big deal. But watch the reaction from your team members when you convey with them that you care about them as humans. Not just as team members.

To be honest, I'm not sure if Bob ever really got comfortable with this one. But he did try at least.

THREE STEP INTO COMPASSION.

We are born compassionate. Compassion is an innately human trait. We start demonstrating compassion in the early months of life.

Compassion is the third part of empathy. After thinking about what it must be like for the other person, and feeling what they must be experiencing. What makes compassion important, and what a lot of people don't understand, is that compassion is about action. It's about doing something for another human who needs support. Sometimes, there's nothing we can do as leaders, but at other times there is.

For Bob, it was very much about understanding what he could do to help. Whether it was approving personal leave when required, working with HR on solutions, or anything else that helped his team to feel cared for.

Fortunately, most (not all, but most) of our coaching clients are open to improving, and to showing up differently. Bob was one of those clients. And of course, his team benefited greatly.

Demonstrate radical candour, and you'll see it yourself. But if you want to see the effects on paper in black and white, there's a way to do that, too: with 360-degree feedback—that's done right.

HOW TO GET 360-DEGREE FEEDBACK SURVEYING RIGHT

For leaders to do their best work, it's important that they get feedback from those around them. From their leader, from their peers, and from their team members. It's important that the feedback is open and honest, and relevant to the leader and the organisation. Unfortunately, it's easy to get the process wrong. As I did in the early days of doing leadership development work.

Here's how to get the process right, so that the leaders get a tonne of value from the process.

ONE GET THE PREPARATION RIGHT.

This part of the process is crucial. It sets the process, and sets the leader up for success. You need to remember that feedback can be confronting for some people, so the more information that you give them about why you're doing the survey, the better. An explanatory meeting or email should go out at least a week before the survey with an overview of how the process will work, and why it's being done. And it should focus on the fact that the survey is being done with the right intent, to support the personal and professional development of the leaders.

Part of the preparation process is to let the leaders know that the surveyor is going to sit down with each leader and deliver the survey results, to help interpret and understand them, and to ensure the leaders know that the survey will be done anonymously. This last point is key, as the feedback needs to be de-identified.

Continue your preparation with getting the questions right. Make sure the questions are focused on your organisation's values and vision. This is so the leader can be made aware of how they're living those values, or if they have some opportunities for improvement.

Once you get the questions right, you can set up the survey. How you develop the survey will make or break the success of the process. That's because the questions need to make sense and be relevant to those completing the survey. The survey needs to be easily accessible and easy to complete, including both multiple choice questions, and free text questions. Then it needs to be sent to the leader's leader, their peers, and their team members, so the surveyor can collect and collate the information. A note here: more survey responses are not always better. Aim for between ten and fifteen responses, as that's a manageable number. Also allow for one to three respondents not providing enough information on the survey.

TWO GET THE PEOPLE PART RIGHT.

You need to get the people part right, and this is about delivering the survey results. Yes, this is set up for success in the preparation stage of the process; and yes, leaders are still wary as they come into meetings with the surveyor (me) to talk through their survey results.

The biggest 'don't' here is to give leaders 360-degree survey feedback without an explanation, and without giving them the time to understand and process the information. In my experience, leaders come into that meeting not knowing what to expect, and they leave having learnt some valuable information about how those around them perceive their leadership style. And that's worth gold.

And, if you do 360-degree surveying with me and The Guinea Group, we'll catch up again for a quick touch-base after two weeks, to further unpack or talk through the feedback, after the leader has had more time to process the information. Winner.

THREE GET THE POST-PROCESS RIGHT.

Close out the process properly. This involves thanking all respondents for their input. Meeting with the CEO or the other senior leaders, to talk through how the process went. And making sure that overall, all leaders got great value and great information from the 360-degree survey process.

And, if the business is smart, they could ask the surveyor for some feedback on what the main areas of opportunity are (de-identified, of course) overall. And then consider if a training or coaching process is required to further support the leaders and their development.

This is a part of the work we do. Yes, 360-degree surveying is a great tool to help leaders continue to learn about themselves and develop their skills. Yes, it needs to be done correctly and the business needs to get it right—like all processes, if you get it wrong you can do more harm than good, so do it properly. And yes, it's a great way to see the impact of your leadership, and your commitment to demonstrating radical candour for the benefit of your team members, your organisation, and your development as a leader.

ACTIVITY 3.5
DEMONSTRATE RADICAL CANDOUR

Take some time now to think about what you've learnt in the last chapter.

The series of questions on the following pages will encourage you to think about how you can use radical candour in your leadership, and in the process of uplifting your team.

Alternatively, sit and write about how you feel when you're challenged by your team members, and what you can do better to encourage your team members to take interpersonal risks, share ideas, and share information to help your team—without the fear of criticism.

Do you struggle when you're challenged by your team members? Why, or why not?

Do you think your team members feel free to take interpersonal risks without the fear of rejection, resentment, and ridicule? If so, how did you achieve this?

Answer honestly. When your team is sharing information, are you subject to ruinous empathy, manipulative insincerity, or obnoxious aggression?

In your leadership, do you promote respect, welcome curiosity, and acknowledge ideas? Why, or why not?

Is challenger safety 'a thing' in your workplace? If not, how could you make it 'a thing'?

Do you take a 'sunset-first' approach to making difficult decisions? Why, or why not?

In what ways could you create a safe space for your team so they can speak with influence, impact, and inspiration?

Do you think you give your team members the safety to show up and be the best version of themselves?

In what ways can you move from 'I care' to showing you care for your team?

How effective is your process of obtaining feedback? How could you better conduct 360-degree feedback surveying?

AFTERWORD

If you're still with me, congratulations on making it this far. And thanks for finding me engaging enough that you decided not to put this book down and never look at it again.

What I hope has kept you connected to my words is the radical candour with which I wrote them. I hope you can see how investing in challenger safety and creating a psychologically safe workplace can help you to get the best out of your team—both in KPIs, and in job satisfaction, for the people at every level of your organisation.

I also hope you can see how taking the time to facilitate and allocate tasks to your team members—and letting go of old habits like micromanaging— makes your work life easier in the long run. And how being more attuned to your C-suite team not only improves your capacity to succeed, but creates an atmosphere of judgement-free communication that improves your team's capacity for innovation.

This book isn't the answer to all of your leadership woes. But it's the beginning of the process. A process that needs to start from within, by understanding your own thinking, emotions, and behaviour. So that what you say is what you do, and your team respects you all the more for it.

If you're an old-school leader, the one that I wrote this book for, congratulations on getting through a book you probably weren't comfortable reading. See how helping, not harming, and hearing, not hurting, can make it your team feel valued, cared for, and empowered?

If you're a new-age leader, the one that I wrote this book for, congratulations on getting through a book you probably thought was going to be a lot less work. See how not committing the cardinal sin of leadership is just as effective in building a psychologically safe team as showing your team members that you care about them?

There's a lot more to learn. Go and get stuck into whatever piques your interest: getting 360-degree feedback to improve your leadership; how to deal with leaders who go BOOM when things go BOOM; and how to create a safe space that's more than psychological safety. This book is the beginning, and as long as you're leading, there shouldn't be an end.

Learn more from me. I have a bunch of books and a team of people who can help you become a better leader. Or don't learn more from me. Learn from anyone whose leadership is inspiring to you in any way. Or anyone whose leadership has caused you to engage in the deficit dialogue dilemma, or witness groupthink, or to decide to never, ever lead your team like they led you. Go learn how to lead with radical candour, and care factor, and enough insight to know when to shamelessly hand over the reigns to someone better qualified or more experienced than you are.

If you don't remember anything I've taught you in this book, remember how it made you feel. If it filled you with hope and optimism, and overwhelmed you with the urge to commit to being a better leader, good. Go do it. If it filled you with dread and shame about how bad your leadership really is, good. Go get better at it.

Either way, you got this far because you're becoming reflective. You're learning how to think differently. You're learning how to react differently. You're learning how to answer the big questions—including why you're a leader, and why you do what you do.

Congratulations on finishing this book. You're uplifting your team. Keep going, and you'll soon be enjoying their success—and yours.

REFERENCES

1. Chopra, D. (2010). *The Soul of Leadership: Unlocking Your Potential for Greatness*. Harmony Books.

2. Clark, T. (2019). *The 4 Stages of Psychological Safety: Defining the Path to Inclusion and Innovation*. Berrett-Koehler Publishers.

3. Dweck, C. S. (2006). *Mindset: The New Psychology of Success*. Random House.

4. Edmondson, A. C. (2019). Psychological Safety: The History, Renaissance, and Future of an Interpersonal Construct. *Annual Review of Organizational Psychology and Organizational Behavior, 6*(1), 1-23.

5. Edmondson, A. C. (1999). Psychological Safety and Learning Behavior in Work Teams. *Administrative Science Quarterly, 44*(2), 350-383.

6. Goleman, D. (1995). *Emotional Intelligence: Why It Can Matter More Than IQ*. New York, NY: Bantam Books.

7. Jaques, E. (1998). *Requisite Organization: A Total System for Effective Managerial Organization and Managerial Leadership for the 21st Century*. Cason Hall & Co Publishers.

8. LaPorte, T. R. (1996). High Reliability Organizations: Unlikely, Demanding and At Risk. *Journal of Contingencies and Crisis Management, 4*(2), 60-71.

9. Lencioni, P. (2002). *The Five Dysfunctions of a Team: A Leadership Fable*. Jossey-Bass.

10. MacDonald, C., Burke, S., & Stewart, K. (2013). *Systems Leadership: Creating Positive Organisations*. Bristol University Press.

11. Paulhus, D. L., & Williams, K. M. (2002). The dark triad of personality: Narcissism, Machiavellianism, and psychopathy. *Journal of research in personality, 36*(6), 556-563.

12. Scott, K. (2017). *Radical Candor: Be a Kick-Ass Boss Without Losing Your Humanity*. St. Martin's Press.

13. Sinek, S. (2011). *Start With Why: How Great Leaders Inspire Everyone to Take Action*. Portfolio.

14. Vasconcellos, E. (2021, March 31). *6 Types of Office 'Politicians' and How to Handle Them*. Business News Daily. Retrieved from https://www.businessnewsdaily.com/3048-coping-office-politics.html

GLOSSARY

Akratic. Characterised by a weakness of will, resulting in action against one's better judgement.

Allocation. A consultative process of assigning tasks and responsibilities involving engagement, discussion and agreement between leaders and their team members (as opposed to delegation).

Amygdala hijack. Coined by psychologist Daniel Goleman. Where processing emotions such as fear, anger, and anxiety, overrides the prefrontal cortex, the part of the brain responsible for reasoning and decision making.

Avoidant-focused coping. A style of coping where the person pretends the event or stressor doesn't exist and avoids dealing with it.

Bandwidth (leadership and management). The capacity or limit of an individual or team to effectively lead and manage a certain number of people, projects, or responsibilities.

Big 3 leadership mandates. The obligations of leaders to the organisation, to the team, and to the self. Also known as values, transformation, and control (VTC).

BOOM Event. An unexpected serious or catastrophic event in the workplace or the lives of an organisation's employees.

Bystander effect. Psychological phenomenon where the inhibiting influence of the presence of others affects a person's willingness to help someone in need.

Care factor. Strategy for effective leadership involving giving team members time, using conversation techniques around psychological safety, psychological empowerment, and psychological connection, and being courageous in the process.

CBT. Cognitive Behavioural Therapy. A form of psychological treatment or therapy that focuses on changing negative or unhelpful thoughts and behaviours in order to improve mental health and wellbeing.

Challenger safety. One of the four stages of psychological safety in teams in Timothy R Clark's theory on how safe team members feel to speak up, and offer ideas, opinions, and views without the fear of resentment, ridicule, or rejection.

Conscious control. The ability to intentionally and actively regulate one's thoughts, emotions, and behaviours using conscious awareness and decision-making processes. Includes emotional, behavioural, and situational control.

Conscious leadership. A leadership approach that emphasises self-awareness, personal growth, and the cultivation of positive relationships and organisational culture. Conscious leaders are aware of their own thoughts, feelings, and behaviours, and how they affect others, and create a supportive, inclusive, and purpose-driven workplace.

C-Suite team. The group of top executives in an organisation (usually including the CEO, COO, CFO, CMO, CTO, and CHRO) who are responsible for setting the strategic direction of the organisation, making major decisions, and overseeing the day-to-day operations of the business to achieve its goals and objectives.

Dark Triad. A psychological term to describe three personality traits that are characterised by a lack of empathy, a tendency toward exploitative behaviour, and a focus on self-interest and personal gain. Comprised of three traits including narcissism, machiavellianism, and psychopathy. Associated with negative outcomes in personal and professional relationships, and in mental health and wellbeing.

Delegation. A process of assigning tasks and responsibilities to team members without collaboration with or input from their leader.

Deficit dialogue dilemma. A term to describe the challenge of effectively communicating and building understanding across different perspectives and worldviews in an organisation. Arises when individuals or groups with differing viewpoints are unable or unwilling to engage in productive dialogue with one another due to factors such as ideological polarisation, social or cultural barriers, or a lack of trust or respect between groups, leading to a breakdown in communication, a lack of cooperation and collaboration, and organisational dysfunction.

DiSC profile. A personality assessment tool designed to help individuals understand their behavioural preferences and communication styles. The DiSC model categorises people into four primary behavioural styles: Dominance (direct and assertive communication style and focus on results), Influence (persuasive and enthusiastic communication style and focus on building relationships), Steadiness (patient and supportive communication style focused on collaboration), and Conscientiousness (a cautious communication style and focus on quality and accuracy).

Disciplined courage. The courage you need to stand up for your position and maintain your commitments when things are going badly.

Duress. Wrongful or unlawful coercion applied by another person (usually a leader). Distinct from normal stress, strain or pressure.

EI (also EQ). Theory of emotional intelligence heavily influenced by Daniel Goleman. Applied in profiling tools to assess social management on measures of empathy, sensitivity, and appreciation; service, compassion, and benevolence; holistic communication; situational perceptual awareness; and interpersonal development.

Emotion-focused coping. A type of stress management that attempts to reduce negative emotional responses associated with stress. Negative emotions such as embarrassment, fear, anxiety, depression, excitement, and frustration are reduced or removed by various coping methods.

Empathetic courage. The courage to challenge your personal biases so you're better placed to experience what others are going through and to understand why.

Empathy. The key skill for leading under pressure. A process beginning with cognitive understanding of what someone is going though, and ending with doing something (where possible) to support them.

Golden Rule (of communication). Treating others how you would want to be treated.

Groupthink. A phenomenon that occurs when a group of individuals reaches a consensus without critical reasoning or evaluation of the consequences or alternatives.

Growth Mindset. A concept popularised by psychologist Carol Dweck. A belief that individuals can develop their abilities and intelligence through hard work, dedication, and perseverance, and that talents and abilities are not fixed, but can be improved through effort and learning.

High Reliability Organisation (HRO). An organisation that operates in complex, high-risk environments where the consequences of errors can be severe (e.g. nuclear power plants, air traffic control centres, and hospitals). Characterised by a strong safety culture, a commitment to continuous improvement, and a focus on identifying and managing risks.

Intellectual courage. The courage you need to turn your knowledge into action in the workplace.

Lencioni Model. A popular leadership development and team-building framework developed by author and consultant Patrick Lencioni. Provides a clear and actionable roadmap for building effective teams, involving trust, productive conflict, commitment, accountability, and a focus on achieving outcomes and results through both individual effort and collaboration.

LMX (Leader-Member Exchange). A leadership theory that focuses on the relationship between a leader and their individual followers or team members. Suggests that the quality of the relationship between a leader and their team members can have a significant impact on individual and team performance.

Manipulative Insincerity. Insincerity in your responses, feedback or praises, without the sugar-coating, that's delivered with the intent to hurt or harm.

Metacognition. Described as 'thinking about thinking.' How you learn and gain knowledge, and then how you apply that knowledge.

Normal Accident Theory. A theory the field of system safety engineering that explains why complex technological systems are susceptible to catastrophic failures or accidents. Suggests that accidents are an inevitable result of the complexity and interconnectedness of modern technological systems, and that no amount of planning, engineering, or design can completely eliminate the possibility of an accident occurring.

Obnoxious Aggression. Being clear, but not kind (also known as 'brutal honesty'), and unlike manipulative insincerity. Unintentionally causes hurt through poor delivery of the message.

Platinum rule (of communication). Communicating with others in the communication style they prefer, not the style you prefer.

PR6. The six elements of resilience developed by Jurie Rossouw. Includes vision, collaboration, composure, health, tenacity, and reasoning.

Problem-focused coping. Addressing the root cause of a stressor, and taking ownership and responsibility for either solving or minimising the problem with whatever resources are available at the time.

Project Aristotle. A research project initiated by Google in 2012 to study what makes a successful team. Identifies key factors that contribute to high-performing teams and improve team effectiveness and productivity, including psychological safety, dependability, structure and clarity, meaning, and impact.

Psychological safety. A concept describing the extent to which team members feel that they are respected, valued, and that their contributions are important, and how safe and comfortable they feel expressing their thoughts, ideas, and concerns without fear of negative consequences. Encourages open communication, promotes learning and innovation, and can improve team performance.

RACI matrix. A project management tool used to define and clarify roles and responsibilities within a team. RACI stands for Responsible, Accountable, Consulted, and Informed. The matrix is used to assign these roles to team members for each task or activity in a project.

Radical candour. A leadership approach that allows and encourages team members to share ideas and information, and contributes to the psychological safety of the workplace.

Ruinous Empathy. Insincerity in responses, feedback, or praises, and sugar-coating of criticism, to avoid the other person feeling bad.

Siloing. When leaders or team members don't operate as part of a team, but focus on their work, department, or business unit without regard for the rest of the organisation.

Senior leadership team (SLT). Also called Senior leadership group. A team of leaders of different levels that manage the running of the business to help it reach its goals.

Sunset-first approach. Letting the 'sun set' on a major decision or the execution of a major decision, i.e., thinking and 'sleeping on it' before coming back the next day to make a decision.

Systems Leadership. The practice of leading and managing complex systems, such as organisations, by focusing on the interrelationships and interconnectedness of the various components and stakeholders involved. Seeks to engage all members of the system in collaborative problem solving, decision making, and innovation. Requires a range of skills, including communication, collaboration, systems thinking, data analysis, and strategic planning.

Team Charter. A document that outlines the purpose, goals, roles, and expectations of a team so all members have a clear understanding of the team's mission, objectives, and expectations for performance.

Team management systems (TMS). A set of tools and assessments used for profiling and managing teams. Provides a framework for understanding team dynamics and individual preferences, and helps team leaders to identify and leverage the strengths of their team members.

Tell courage. The courage to articulate goals and objectives to the team.

Tepid leadership. A laissez-faire, 'hands-off' approach to leadership where the leader doesn't sufficiently support the team members.

Toxic Workplace Culture. An environment in which employees experience persistent negative attitudes, behaviours, and practices that have a harmful impact on their wellbeing and job performance. Common characteristics include lack of trust, bullying and harassment, poor communication, high levels of stress, lack of recognition and reward, low morale, and resistance to change.

Transactional leadership. A contingent reward-based style of leadership where the leader expects strict compliance with business practice.

Transformational leadership. A process in which leaders and followers help each other to advance to a higher level of morale and motivation.

Trust courage. The courage to trust team members to reach a goal themselves.

Trust-less leadership. Aka micromanagement, where the leader does not allow team members sufficient responsibility and room for professional growth.

Tuckman Model. A widely recognised model in the field of team dynamics developed by psychologist Bruce Tuckman in 1965. Identifies four stages of group development: forming, storming, norming, and performing.

Try Courage. The courage to try and reach a goal despite the risk of failure.

Values, Transformation, and Control (VTC). A theoretical framework developed by Cameron and Quinn in the 1980s to understand organisational change and development. Posits that culture is made up of three main components: values, transformation, and control. Based on these components, organisations can be classified into one of four categories (clan, adhocracy, market, and hierarchy cultures).

360-degree survey feedback. A type of performance appraisal tool that provides an individual with feedback from multiple sources. Feedback is gathered from various sources, including the individual's manager, peers, direct reports, and customers or stakeholders.

5P process for facilitating workshops. Involves purpose (clearly define and share), process (how to run it and what resources are needed), people (who needs to be there), performance (facilitating questions, encouraging conversation, listening and documenting discussion), and polish (close out process to add value to the time the team has committed to the process).

7 states and traits. Skills for effective leadership that include learning, engaging, articulating, demonstration, empathy, resilience, and safety.

OTHER BOOKS
IN THIS SERIES

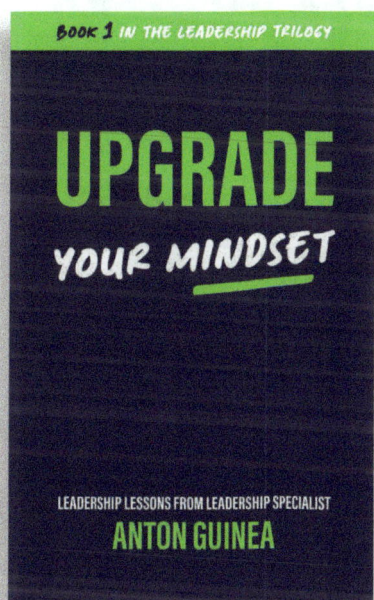

BOOK 1 IN THE LEADERSHIP TRILOGY

UPGRADE
YOUR MINDSET

LEADERSHIP LESSONS FROM LEADERSHIP SPECIALIST
ANTON GUINEA

BOOK 2 IN THE LEADERSHIP TRILOGY

UPSKILL
YOUR LEADERSHIP

LEADERSHIP LESSONS FROM LEADERSHIP SPECIALIST
ANTON GUINEA

Learn how to introspect, put things in perspective, and cope better under pressure as a leader by upgrading your mindset.

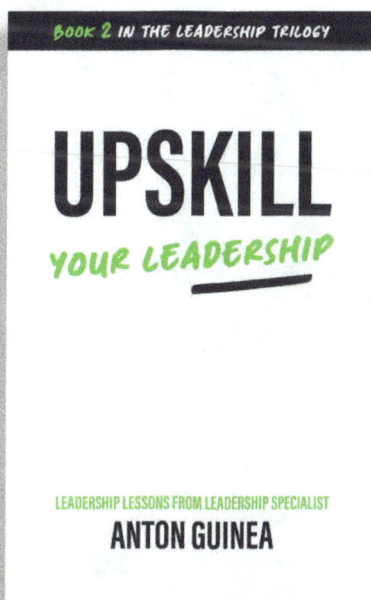

Learn how to create conscious control, develop emotional intelligence, and operate with care factor to upskill your leadership.

ABOUT *ANTON*

Anton's life and work experiences have led him to become a visionary thought leader, delivering the right mix of empathy and enthusiasm in all his programs. His energy, engagement, and enterprise thinking is helping leaders develop into transformational and inspiring role models, who uplift the people in their care, and create high-performing teams.

Anton is a widely regarded keynote speaker. But he is also a qualified Resilience Coach, and a graduate of psychology and human resources. He's supported by The Guinea Group team of professionals, who share his commitment to service and over-delivering for leaders and organisations within Australia and across the world.

This valuable experience, paired with his unshakeable commitment to his 'why'—leaving people better than he found them—underpins his truly transformative programs.

LOOKING FOR A
WORLD-CLASS SPEAKER
FOR YOUR NEXT LIVE OR VIRTUAL LEADERSHIP EVENT?

A professional speaker since 2005, Anton has worked with global organisations within Australia and across the world.

With a noteworthy ability to help people to think differently, Anton's speaking packages also comprise pre- and post-event support and resources, helping leaders and their teams to maintain their commitment to growth and development in the lifelong process of upgrading their mindsets.

Anton is a skilled keynote speaker. But he's also a researcher, and a former tradesperson experienced in working under pressure and for poor-performing leaders. This valuable experience, paired with his unshakeable commitment to his 'why'—leaving people better than he found them—underpins his truly transformative performance as a speaker.

To find out more about how Anton can help you to find your purpose, and to build a meaningful and rewarding career, visit us here.

ANTON GUINEA

www.ingramcontent.com/pod-product-compliance
Lightning Source LLC
Chambersburg PA
CBHW072147020426
42334CB00018B/1914